Uncle John's® THE ENCHANTED TOILET

BATHROOM READER FOR KIDS ONLY!

by the Bathroom Readers' Institute

D1316972

Bathroom Re:
Ashland, Oregon

UNCLE JOHN'S THE ENCHANTED TOILET BATHROOM READER® FOR KIDS ONLY

Copyright © 2012 by Bathroom Readers' Press
(a division of Portable Press). All rights reserved. No part
of this book may be used or reproduced in any manner
whatsoever without written permission, except in the case
of brief quotations embodied in critical articles or reviews.

"Bathroom Reader" is a federally registered trademark
of Bathroom Readers' Press. "Uncle John" is
a trademark of Bathroom Readers' Press.

For information, write:
Bathroom Readers' Institute
P.O. Box 1117, Ashland, OR 97520
www.bathroomreader.com

Cover concept by John Gaffey.
Cover design by Michael Brunsfeld, San Rafael, CA
(*Brunsfeldo@comcast.net*)
Cover illustration by John Gaffey and Michael Brunsfeld.
Interior design by Helen Robinson.
Folio illustration by Patrick Merrell.

ISBN-10: 1-60710-558-6 / ISBN-13: 978-1-60710-558-9

Library of Congress Cataloging-in-Publication Data
Uncle John's the enchanted toilet bathroom reader for kids only
     p. cm.
  ISBN 978-1-60710-558-9 (pbk.)
1. Curiosities and wonders—Juvenile literature. 2. Fantasy
fiction—Miscellanea. 3. Magic—Miscellanea. I. Bathroom
Readers' Institute (Ashland, Or.)
  AG243.U48 2012
  031.02—dc23

                                    2011053136

Printed in the United States of America
First Printing

17 16 15 14 13 12   6 5 4 3 2 1

READERS RAVE

Some books print fancy reviews written by fancy book critics. Borrring! At the BRI, we care more about what our faithful readers have to say.

"The Bathroom Readers are the most interesting and coolest things around. You guys should win an award!!!"
—**Jennifer S.**

"I inadvertently stole one from my teacher. (Sorry Mr. Mont!) I got hooked, my family got hooked, and now I have my nieces and nephews hooked!"
—**Michael C.**

"I remember reading the first *Bathroom Reader* as a kid, and learning that Barbie had a last name. (Roberts!)"
—**Katie F.**

"I love your books! I have eleven books. I take them to school and everyone loves to read them. "
—**Andrew S.**

"Waassssuuuupppp! I just wanted to shout out to all the cool dudes and chicas working on the Bathroom Reader staff! I became totally addicted to the BRs last year when my mom gave the thirteenth edition to my dad for Christmas! My life hasn't been the same since!"
—**Kim B.**

THANK YOU

The Bathroom Readers' Institute sincerely thanks the people whose advice and assistance made this book possible.

Gordon Javna

Kim T. Griswell

Trina Hedgpeth

Jay Newman

Brian Boone

Michael Brunsfeld

Rich Wallace

Carly Schuna

Kelly Milner Halls

Nancy Coffelt

John Gaffey

Valeri Gorbachev

John O'Brien

Will Strong

Michelle R. Weaver

Patrick Merrell

Joan M. Kyzer

J. Carroll

Melinda Allman

True Sims

JoAnn Padgett

Monica Maestas

Mana Monzavi

Annie Lam

Sydney Stanley

Lilian Nordland

Ginger Winters

Jennifer Frederick

RR Donnelley

Publishers Group West

The Evo's Gang

Thomas Crapper

TABLE OF CONTENTS

CASTLES & KINGDOMS
Moat, Moat...
   What's in the Moat?...36
Take That! 49
Musical Ghosts..............66
Real-Life Princesses 90
The Well-Dressed
   Knight 240

BOOK MAGIC
Wizard Schools 15
U.J.'s Guide to
   Enchanted Places........174
The Boy Who Loved
   Dragons 176
And the Magic
   Number Is..................195
Grim Tales from the
   Brothers Grimm 220

DRAGONS & KNIGHTS
Dragon Domains............24
Everyday Knight Facts...28
Dragon Sightings.........108

Sir John's Guide to Taming
   Your Dragon 259

ENCHANTED HISTORY
Confucious and
   the Unicorn.................46
Confucious Said 115
Make Mine Mead..........93
King Arthur's
   Mystical Isle..............119

FABULOUS FAIRIES
Odd Fairy Lore 12
Fairy Surprises...............75
Disappearing Fairy
   Finger Puppets..........110
Fairy-Dust Wishes 138
Do You Believe?............215
Fairy Identification
   Guide 275

GIGGLES & RIDDLES
Castle Crackups 11
Riddle Me This! 32

The White Queen's
   Riddle 64
Fairy Tale
   Tongue Twisters.......... 98
Confucius Didn't Say... 116
Mother Goosed 236
Witch Wit 278

GRAPHIC TALES

Little Miss Muffett......... 17
The Three Silly Huntsmen
   (on Safari) 33
Jack and the Bean Dog .. 52
The Tall Tall Tower 81
The Fairy Hedgehog 104
Cockroach and the
   Household Pests 121
The Three Silly Huntsmen
   (Go Fishing) 134
The Enchanted Toilet... 152
Bet and the Beauty 171
The Hairstory of
   Rapunzel................... 197
Cider Ella 216
Chicken Big 237
The Three Silly Huntsmen
   (at the North Pole)... 271

MAGICAL CREATURES

Beastly Origins 127
Little-Known
   Little Folk 147
Burn, Birdie, Burn!....... 164
Know Your Mythical
   Beasts 257

MAGICAL MISCHIEF

Gremlins' Guide.............20
Wizard Headgear........... 43
Play Ogre Oblivion........56
Ridiculous!....................58
The Wandmaker's
   Workshop 114
How to Bamboozle
   a Troll....................... 230
A Pox Upon Thee!.......285

THE SECRET ARTS

How to Make
   a Wish 86
Bag of Runes 92
Color Power 125
Who's Scrying Now? ... 145
Movie Magic............... 166
In a Trance 202
Bathroom Readers'
   Tarot........................ 206

Tell Fortunes
 with Runes 250
Secret Arts
 of the Ninjas............. 261

STRANGE SCIENCE
Fun Facts About Farts .. 80
Turn Lead into Gold 94
Vanishing Cloak......... 103
Alchemical Facts
 and Fakes................. 184
Color Alchemy 185
Common Cents........... 279

TWISTED TALES
Three Mooned Mice 13
Goldilocks and the Three
 Puffer Fish 21
The Pudding Cake Man .. 30
The Shoemaker and the
 Elvis Impersonators 39
The Three Little
 Jackalopes...................44
Hoard It!
 The Tooth Fairy.........50
The Legend of
 Bluebeard.................... 61
The Fairy Gamemaster....68
The Fart King............... 77

K-9ery Row 87
Socked In 99
Stinking Beauty 111
Outfoxed 117
The Loch Ness
 Prankster 130
The Wolf Girl 140
The Milkmaid's
 Halloween 149
Dumb Cluck................ 160
The Boy Who Cried
 Celebrity................... 168
The Pie Piper............... 178
Rotten Robin and His
 Scary Wrens.............. 192
The Hare's Side of
 the Story....................209
The Princess and
 the Peashooter.......... 223
Tikki Tikki Who? 232
Magically Delicious 243
The Emperor's New
 Underwear................. 253
The Platypus Prince....266
Ali Baba and the
 Forty Steves.............. 281

Warts & Wizards

A Visit to the Witch
   Doctor 42
Brazil's Forest Guardians .. 59
Soccer Sorcery 72
Ha! Craven Knight 85
Witches' Brews 142
Hogwarts: An Insider's
   Guide 158
Weird Wizards 182
Who Was that Merlin
   Guy Anyway? 187
Witch Hunts 212
Have Broom,
   Will Travel 227
Enchanted Education .. 247

Yum's the Word

Witchy Snacks 27
Syllabubble Without
   the Trouble 65
The Magic Teakettle 101
Treats to Catch
   a Leprechaun 132
How to Attract an Elf ... 162

The Answers

For Checking
   (or Peeking) 286

*Meet Jack and the
Bean Dog on page 25.*

ENCHANTED GREETINGS FROM UNCLE JOHN

Not long ago, in a little red house not far away (if you live in Oregon), I nodded off in my chair and started to dream. Because very odd things happen in dreams, I fell into a fractured fairy tale about the three little pigs. (For you history buffs, the actual cartoon aired in 1961 on *The Bullwinkle Show*.)

AND NOW, BACK TO MY DREAM...

I hid behind the door as a messenger delivered a singing telegram to three plump pig sisters. "Put on the skillet. Put on the lid. Your rich uncle just wound up dead!" sang the messenger. The pig sisters celebrated being rich beyond their wildest dreams by building fancy houses. And I laughed so hard I fell out of my chair and landed on my head. "Eureka!" I shouted. "Totally twisted fairy tales!"

A few seconds later, a wizard knocked on the front door. Before I could say "Stop waving that wand at m—" the book you're holding in your hands—*The Enchanted Toilet*—went from an idea in my throbbing head to... the book you're holding in your hands.

By now, you may be wondering: Why is Uncle John babbling on about his dreams and a wizard and an

enchanted toilet? Good question! It's because this is
not your usual *Uncle John's Bathroom Reader for Kids
Only*. Flip through the pages and you'll find dragon lairs,
wizard schools, edible eyeballs, gremlins, and a Chinese
philosopher talking to a unicorn. You'll also find more
than two dozen totally twisted fairy tales, *plus* thirteen
fully illustrated graphic twisted tales. And they're all
guaranteed to make you laugh hard enough to fall off
whatever throne you're sitting on and land on your...
head.

By the way, that annoying little fairy flitting around the
page? That's the fart fairy. If anything in this book really
stinks—the jokes, for example—it's his fault. He flew in
through the bathroom window and started zapping one
page after another. We couldn't stop him, so we turned
him into a game called "Find the Fart Fairy." To play, all
you have to do is count how many times the fart fairy
appears in the book. Then turn to page 286 and discover
your reward. (No peeking, or I'll send the fart fairy to
your house.)

May all your toilets be enchanted...

Go with the flow!

—Uncle John

CASTLE CRACKUPS

A few chuckles from the medieval kings of comedy.

Q: Why did the prince hate math class?
A: Because he had to cram-a-lot.

Q: Why did Sir Sleepy buy a new horse?
A: His old horse was a knight mare.

Q: Why did the king fall off his chair?
A: He was throne for a loop.

Q: What do you call a knight who can't stop emailing?
A: Sir Spam-a-lot.

Q: What was Merlin's favorite school subject?
A: Spelling.

Q: Sir Gallopsalot rode to the castle on Friday, stayed three days, and then left on Friday. How was that possible?
A: His horse's name was Friday.

Q: Why did Prince Practical have holes in his undies?
A: So he could get his feet through them.

Q: Which six letters did the queen mutter when she saw that the royal treasury was bare?
A: "O-Y-R-U-M-T?"

Q: What did the dragon say when it saw knights guarding the castle?
A: "Oh, no! Canned food."

Odd Fairy Lore

When it comes to fairies, people will believe almost anything.
Here are some of the stranger documented beliefs.

- Fairies protect nature and grant favors to humans who are kind to animals and use nontoxic cleaning supplies.
- Fairies collect treasures humans lose. One kind of fairy specializes in drains. Drain fairies tend to be smelly, but they have huge collections of rings, earrings, and contact lenses.
- *Blinks* are fairies for the modern world. Blinks believe that every machine has a creature trapped inside it, forced to serve its human owners. Their job? To free the creatures. (So if your computer stops working…)
- Fairies consider the word "fairy" an insult. Using the word has led to shipwrecks, baby kidnappings, and an outbreak of mad cow disease. These names are "safe" to use: *the hill people, the gentry, the wee folk, the good neighbors,* and *the people of peace.*
- Passing troops of fairies cause whirlwinds. They can carry away souls, crops, and people. If you spot a whirlwind, lie down on the ground until it passes.
- Fart faires cause methane gas levels in drinking water to rise. In Texas, a water safety official is rumored to have said, "We have never had a documented case of water contamination from a fart fairy."

THREE MOONED MICE

An Uncle John's Totally Twisted Tale

THREE LITTLE MOUSE BROTHERS were fed up with the farmer's wife. She was scary and mean and needed a taste of her own medicine. "Let's nibble off her toes!" said the first mouse brother.

"That'll teach her," agreed his two brothers.

"Stay away from that woman," their mother warned. "She carries a carving knife wherever she goes, and she loves to use it on mice." She scissored two fingers together. "Snip! Snip! There go your tails." The mouse mother tucked her little ones into their nest in the wall behind the kitchen pantry. Then she kissed their whiskery cheeks. "Just leave that nasty old hag alone."

It was true. The three mouse brothers had seen pink stumps where the tails of careless mice had once been. They would have to be *very* careful.

"We need a plan," one brother said.

"A safe one!" said the second.

"We need a place where she won't bring the knife," said the third.

"I know!" said the first mouse. "The shower! We can sneak up to the bathroom and ambush her there."

"Perfect!" said the third mouse.

"She'll never expect it!" said the second.

"What could go wrong?" squealed the first.

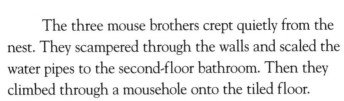

The three mouse brothers crept quietly from the nest. They scampered through the walls and scaled the water pipes to the second-floor bathroom. Then they climbed through a mousehole onto the tiled floor.

The farmer's wife was already in the shower. Steam filled the room. The three mice crept forward on silent mouse paws. But just as they whipped open the shower curtain, the farmer's wife dropped the soap and bent over to pick it up.

"Help!" cried the first mouse, blinded by the full moon of the farmer's wife's backside.

"My eyes!" cried the second.

"I can't see!" cried the third.

The three blinded mice scrambled to escape. They raised such a clatter they didn't hear the farmer's wife exit the shower and reach for her carving knife. *Thunk!* The knife slammed down on the floor, slicing into a tile.

"Run!" shouted the first mouse.

They pinged and ponged around the room, trying to find the mousehole. Just as the knife started to come down again, they tumbled through the opening, narrowly escaping with their tails—and their lives.

"Have you ever seen such a sight in your life?" asked the first mouse brother as they crept back into the nest.

"Never," said the second.

"Thank goodness we're blind," said the third. "We won't ever have to see it again."

THE END

WIZARD SCHOOLS

Did J.K. Rowling steal the ideas for Harry Potter? Probably not, but these fictional wizard schools existed long before Hogwarts, and the details sound…awfully familiar.

THE UNSEEN UNIVERSITY

In 1983, fourteen years before Harry got his invitation to Hogwarts, author Terry Pratchett created the Unseen University for his Discworld novels. One character is a budding wizard with rumpled black hair who wears round black glasses. (Hmm…)

    The professors at the Unseen University are lazy, inept old wizards who like to gossip and eat a lot. In fact, people regularly donate food to the school. Why? They want to keep the daft old magicians too full to move. That way they won't be tempted to rip holes in reality. The school's motto? "Eta Beta Pi" (Eat a Better Pie).

THE ARCHMAGE'S SCHOOL

Ursula K. Le Guin's *A Wizard of Earthsea* was published in 1984. The story follows a young magician named Ged who arrives at the Archmage's school on the island of Roke. Ged has a chip on his shoulder and a seriously swollen ego. After all, he can conjure up storms, transform himself into a hawk, split rock, and even talk to dragons. To impress the other students, Ged summons a spirit, but his plan backfires. The evil shadow

overpowers him, and the Archmage must step forward to drive it away. The headmaster is so weakened by the battle that he dies. (Hmm, that *also* sounds familiar.)

WIZARD'S HALL

What about this story line? A shy boy named Henry heads off to Wizard's Hall, where the pictures on the walls *actually move*. Henry befriends a red-haired boy and a brilliant studious girl, goes awry with some of his early spells, and rises to excellence in a battle against an evil wizard and his soul-stealing beast. Henry's not an orphan; his mother sends him to Wizard's Hall. And he's not "the chosen one," merely one of 113 talented wizards called to battle the evil wizard, Nettle. Still, author Jane Yolen published *Wizard's Hall* in 1991, *six years* before Harry Potter set off for Hogwarts.

THE WRITING WIZARDS SPEAK

- **Terry Pratchett says:** "As soon as the Harry Potter boom began, journalists who hadn't read a children's book in years went, 'Wow, a wizards' school! Wow, broomstick lessons!' I, of course, used a time machine to 'get the idea' of Unseen University from Hogwarts."
- **Ursula K. Le Guin says:** "I didn't feel Rowling ripped me off. My incredulity was at the critics who found the first book wonderfully original. She has many virtues, but originality isn't one of them."
- **Jane Yolen says:** "If Ms. Rowling would like to cut me a very large check, I would cash it."

LITTLE MISS MUFFET
BY MICHELLE R. WEAVER

BRAVE HUNTER NEEDED

LITTLE MISS MUFFET SAT ON HER TUFFET—

EATING HER CURDS AND WHEY.

WHEN ALONG CAME A SPIDER—

AHEM

WHO CRAWLED UP BESIDE HER—

GREMLINS' GUIDE

Gremlins are mischievous beasties that mess up machines. During World War II, pilots often blamed them for sabotaging planes. These days, they like to crash computers. Want to be a gremlin? Try these tricks!

1. AUTO INCORRECT
The AutoCorrect option in word processing programs will replace any word with any other word. Set Auto-Correct to replace a common word like "Sir" with something silly like "Smelly Sock." From then on, Auto-Correct will change "Dear Sir" to "Dear Smelly Sock."

2. SHRIEKING CELL PHONES!
Go to a cell phone's sound setting. Choose the most annoying ringer sound. Then turn up the volume.

3. SCREEN SHOCKER
Add some scary photos to a computer's desktop photos. Set the photos to change every five minutes.

4. GOOFY EMAIL GREETING
Go into an email program's settings. In the "Compose" section, look for "Greeting Name." Type in a silly name, such as "Ura Fruitcake." Save the change. The next time the email program is opened, the greeting message will read, "Good morning, Ura Fruitcake!"

GOLDILOCKS AND THE THREE PUFFER FISH

....

An Uncle John's Totally Twisted Tale

FOR YEARS, PEOPLE HAVE SPREAD the story of a little girl named Goldilocks. She sneaks into a house where three bears live, eats their food, breaks their chairs, and falls asleep in the smallest bear's bed. What a fairy tale!

Goldilocks's *real* story took place in Atlantis, where a family of mutant puffer fish lived in an undersea castle. Papa Puffer Fish was the size of a hot-air balloon. Mama Puffer Fish was the size of a beach ball, and Baby Puffer Fish was the size of a super ball—you know, those little bouncy things that roll under the sofa and can never be found again?

Anyway, Goldilocks was a skilled SCUBA diver. For months she'd been on a quest to discover the lost city of Atlantis. During one dive, she spotted the puffer fish family's underwater castle.

Goldie's crew was on the deck of her ship, *The Naughahyde*, watching the dive via her helmet cam.

"Going in!" Goldilocks signaled.

The inside of the castle was magnificent. Goldilocks floated into the first room, where she found three chairs made of calcified coral. She tried to sit in the first one. "Geez!" she said. "Whoever sits in this chair must have a butt the size of a hot-air balloon." The second chair was smaller, but it was still too big for Goldie's tush. The third chair was...just right. But when Goldie sat down, the weird round depression in the middle of the chair—about the size of a super ball—made it very uncomfortable.

So Goldilocks swam to the next room, where she found three bowls of seaweed stew. The first bowl would have served a blue whale. The second, a great white shark. So she swam to the third bowl to sample what was inside. "Ew!" She took off her helmet cam and pointed it toward herself so her crew could see that she was holding her nose. "This stuff reeks!"

In the final castle room, Goldilocks found three beds covered with soft sea sponges. The crew members could see the sleepy look in their team leader's eyes.

"Goldie! Don't do it!" they shouted. But Goldilocks turned off the sound on her helmet cam and ignored them.

She sat on the first bed, but it was too hard. "Not enough sponges." She yawned and moved on to the next bed. It was covered in so many sponges that when she flopped down on it, all you could see was the lens on her helmet cam sticking out. "Too fluffy," said Goldie's sponge-muffled voice. The last bed, however, had one perfect layer of sea sponges. "Just right," said Goldie.

As Goldilocks drifted off to sleep, her crew watched in horror. The mutant puffer fish family was swimming toward the castle. (*Bah-dum…Bah-dum.*)

"Get out of there!" they yelled, but Goldie couldn't hear them.

What followed is too terrible to describe.

Really.

We can't talk about it.

Why? Because Goldie's crew sold the video to *America's Most Horrible Fairy-Tale Endings*. The episode airs next season. (Unless the show is canceled, which would be a shame.)

THE END

∘ ∘ ∘

BARELY BEARABLE RIDDLES

Q: What do you call Goldilocks when it's freezing outside?
A: Coldilocks.

Q: What did Goldilocks call her grandmother?
A: Oldylocks.

Q: What do you call Goldilocks when she plays pin the tail on the donkey?
A: Blindfoldilocks.

Q: What do you call Goldilocks's mother when she nags?
A: Scoldilocks.

Q: What do you call Goldilocks when she gets out of jail early?
A: Paroledilocks.

Q: What do you call a zombie Goldilocks?
A: Moldylocks.

DRAGON DOMAINS

Q: Why don't you ever see dragons? A: Because they're hiding!
Here's where people once thought you could find them.

A (RIDICULOUSLY) BRIEF HISTORY

Legends of dragons terrorizing people have been around
for thousands of years. Dragons show up in the ancient
lore of China, Europe, the Middle East, and, more
recently, in the Americas. Over time, rumors spread
that dragons liked to steal treasure, breathe fire, and
eat maidens. Result: Some knight or dragon slayer was
always out to prove himself by finding a dragon and
killing it. So a crafty dragon had to find a place to hole
up. Here are a few legendary lairs.

COOL CAVES. For dragons that loved dark, damp
places, caves made ideal hideouts. A dragon could see
nearby villages from its cave and stay out of sight while
planning attacks. Wawel Hill in Krakow, Poland, is
now crowned by a castle. But before the castle was built
(sometime before A.D. 1100) a dragon was rumored to live
in a cave on the hill's western slope. The name of this
fearsome creature? Smok Wawelski. To avoid the dragon's
wrath, villagers were supposed to leave a certain number
of cattle outside his cave each day. But if "lunch" didn't
show up? Smok stormed out of his cave and gobbled up
an equal number of human heads.

MAJESTIC MOUNTAINS. Flying dragons sought safety in dens near the tops of steep mountains. A dragon could swoop down to steal a cow or a wandering child, and then return to its den to eat. The *Drachenfels* (Dragon Rock) near Bonn, Germany, was the legendary home of a dragon with a very unbalanced diet: It ate only young women. That made it the prime target of a hero named Siegfried. Siegfried climbed up to the dragon's lair, killed it, and then bathed in its blood. (And you thought dragons were vicious!)

WILD WATERS. Serpent-like dragons once lurked in lakes, rivers, and oceans. Thousands of years ago one water dragon, the Carthaginian serpent, supposedly hid out in the reeds of Africa's Bagrada River. When Roman soldiers tried to wade across the river, the dragon squeezed them to death in its terrible coils and then gulped them down. The soldiers fought back. They set up machines to catapult boulders from the riverbank. After several tries, they managed to smash the beast's skull. A general named Regulus sent the dragon's skin home to Rome. It was 120 feet long; that's longer than the blue whale, the largest mammal now living on Earth. The dragon's skin "disappeared" in 322 B.C.

DEEP SWAMPS. In England, swamp dragons—called knuckers—hid out in marshy holes. Knucker holes were so deep the water near the bottom never froze, not even in winter. The swamp gas made a knucker's breath foul

enough to scorch skin right off the bone.

The Dunna Knucker, said to have once lived near Lyminster, West Sussex, liked to eat livestock and people. A boy named Jim Puttock set a trap: he put a poisoned pie in a cart near the knucker's hole. The knucker ate the pie and the cart...and the horse.

o o o

YOUR PET DRAGON

Take this quiz to discover the dragon that's right for you!

1. If bites that can infect and kill you don't matter, go to number 2. If they do, go to number 4.

2. If your parents won't let you keep a 300-pound dragon in your room, go to 4. If they will, go to 3.

3. If you want a 10-foot-long dragon that eats pigs, deer, and the occasional child, go to A. If you want a safer pet, go to 4.

4. If you are willing to wait for scientists to genetically engineer a dragon like the ones you see in movies, go to B. If you want a pet dragon now, go to C.

A. *The Komodo Dragon is for you!* These giant lizards live in Indonesia. (Sorry. They won't let you take one on a plane.)

B. *The GeneDupe Real Dragon is for you!* (Oops! The "scientific article" about this dragon was an April Fools' Day hoax.)

C. *The bearded dragon is for you!* They're real lizards, and they're easy to care for. Buy one at your local pet store.

A WITCHY SNACK

Rumor has it that witches enjoy eating fresh eyeballs.
So, quick! Make a batch of these witch-catching treats.

WHAT YOU NEED:

SUPPLIES
- An adult (not a witch)
- Knife
- Cutting board
- Plate

INGREDIENTS
- 1 Roma tomato
- 2 fresh mini mozzarella balls
- 4 large basil leaves
- 2 green olives
- Olive oil (optional)

WHAT TO DO:

1. Ask the adult to help (or to keep an eye out for witches).

2. Put the tomato, mozzarella, and olives on a cutting board. Slice the narrow top and bottom ends off the tomato. Then slice the rest of the tomato into four even pieces.

3. Cut each mini mozzarella ball and each olive in half. Lay out the basil leaves on a plate.

4. Top each leaf with a tomato slice. Put a mozzarella "eyeball" on top of each tomato slice, and then top each eyeball with an olive "pupil."

5. If you want to really tempt the witches, drizzle eye slime (olive oil) over the snack.

Caution: If there are a lot of witches in your neighborhood, double the recipe!

EVERYDAY KNIGHT FACTS

Knights don't just show up in fairy tales—they're a real part of history. From the late 700s through the 1400s knights were warrior nobles in service to king and country.
Here are a few fascinating facts.

- Knights started their training at age seven. A noble boy bound for knighthood went to a neighboring lord's castle to train as a page. The lady of the castle taught him manners. A priest taught him to read and write. And he learned swordplay—with a wooden sword.

- At age 14, a page could become a squire. He might guard prisoners, care for a knight's armor, and begin to train with real weapons.

- The age for becoming an actual knight? About 21.

- Cleaning armor was a bit like making Shake 'n Bake chicken. A knight (or his squire) tossed the armor into a bag with sand, vinegar, and urine (water was too precious) and gave the bag a good shake.

- Only the richest knights could afford full-body armor. Others wore partial armor to protect critical areas like arms, legs, or shoulders. But a used suit of armor could sometimes be picked up for free. Where? On the battlefield. (Dead knights don't need protection.)

- Knights kept their armor much cleaner than they kept themselves. Until the 1200s, knights never bathed. Why not? They believed that bathing sapped their strength.

- A full set of plate armor could weigh 60 pounds or more. That may sound like a lot, but it wasn't enough to slow most knights. To show off how well he could move, a French knight turned a somersault while wearing a full suit of armor.

- In battle, a knight's armor wasn't the only thing weighing him down. He usually carried a two-edged sword, a dagger, a lance, and a heavy club or battle-axe. Total weight of armor and weapons: 100 pounds. (That's about the same weight soldiers carry today.)

- Wearing armor and falling off your horse while crossing a river? Bad idea. An experienced German knight did it, and he drowned.

- Knights weren't the only ones who needed arms and armor. In 1285, every British male between 15 and 60 had to help keep the peace. The more money a man had, the more arms and armor he was forced to buy. If his land brought in about $20 per year, he had to have an iron breastplate, a mail shirt, a sword, and a knife.

- If nature called, a knight had to remove pieces of his armor. But what if he had to pee in the middle of a battle? With swords swinging and arrows flying, no knight in his right mind would take off his armor. If the need grew too great, the knight peed in his suit.

THE PUDDING-CAKE MAN

An Uncle John's Totally Twisted Tale

ONCE UPON A TIME, a boy who had no idea how to cook got a craving for chocolate. So he decided to bake a chocolate pudding cake. He didn't know the first thing about following directions. His cake ended up wobbly and man-shaped. While it was cooling on the counter, the cake sat up and looked at the boy.

"Hey, kid? Don't you know I'm supposed to be made of gingerbread?" said the pudding-cake man.

The boy blinked. "But I wanted chocolate," he said.

"Look at me!" said the pudding-cake man. "I'm too jiggly to move! There's no way I can stand up or run away."

"Then I guess it's time for dessert." The boy grabbed a big spoon and stuck it into the pudding-cake man, who began oozing molten chocolate.

"GAAAHHH!!!" cried the pudding-cake man.

The boy stuck the chocolaty spoon in his mouth. But—since he knew nothing about cooking—he had forgotten to let the pudding cake cool. So he burned his tongue and the roof of his mouth. "GAAAHHH!!!" said the boy. "Evil cake!"

"Sure, blame it on me," grumbled the pudding-cake man. He stuck his finger in the hole the boy had made and realized that he didn't feel a thing. *Wait a second,* he thought. *I can't feel pain, but I yelled as if I did. Maybe I can run away, even though I don't have muscles or bones!*

He decided to give it a try. While the boy scrambled to fill a glass with cold water, the pudding-cake man wiggled to a standing position. Then he stepped off the pan and wobbled across the countertop. He crouched at the edge, waiting for his chance.

The boy gulped down the water and turned around. "I'll show you who's boss," he began, but the pudding-cake man knew that his time had come.

"HIIII-YAH!" screeched the pudding-cake man (even though he had no vocal cords). In a leap that even a flying squirrel would have admired, he soared off the countertop and stuck to the boy's face.

The boy tried to scream, but his cries were muffled by oozing chocolate pudding. Finally, he managed to pull the pudding-cake man off his face. He yanked open the door and flung the terrifying creature outside. "Go!" he ordered. And the pudding-cake man ran, ran, ran, as fast as he…could…his sides jiggling with evil laughter.

The boy slammed the door and looked at the kitchen. It was a wreck. Pudding blobs were everywhere: on the counter, the cabinets, even the floor. Worse still, for the first time ever, the smell of chocolate made him want to spew chunks.

"That's it," said the boy. "I'm never baking again."

THE END

RIDDLE ME THIS

Solve these nursery-rhyme riddles or be a silly goose.

CHOMPING AT THE BIT
Twenty white horses
Upon a red hill;
Now they tramp,
Now they champ,
Now they stand still.

THIS GIRL IS HOT!
Little Nancy Etticoat,
In a white petticoat,
And a red nose;
The longer she stands,
The shorter she grows.

THE YOLK IS ON YOU
No doors there are on this stronghold,
Yet thieves break in and steal the gold.

TUG OF WATER
As round as an apple,
As deep as a cup,
All the king's horses
Can't pull it up.

Answers on page 286.

Three Silly Huntsmen

by Valeri Gorbachev

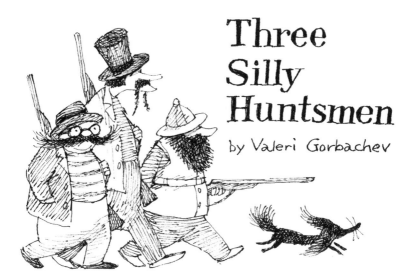

After a long day on safari, three silly huntsmen were awoken by a terrible noise.

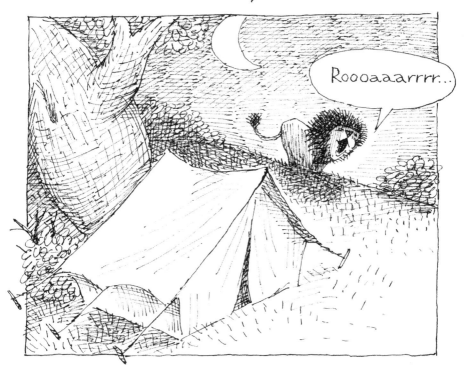

Roooaaarrrr...

MOAT, MOAT...
WHAT'S IN THE MOAT?

Before you start swimming in a castle's moat, you might want to know what's been found floating around in them.

KNIGHT DEFENDS KING

Bodiam Castle near Robertsbridge in East Sussex is one of Great Britain's most famous castles. It was built more than 600 years ago by Sir Edward Dalyngrigge, a knight who served England during the Hundred Years' War.

The Hundred Years' War, by the way, started in 1337 and ended in 1453. This seems to prove that a) the French and English had a hard time getting along in those days, and b) people in the Middle Ages weren't very good at math.

ROOK TAKES CASTLE

Sir Edward must have been quite a knight. He returned from France with so much plunder he needed a castle to show it all off. But he couldn't just start building. First he had to secure his king's permission. How did Sir Edward convince King Richard II that he needed a castle? He told the king that the castle would keep the French from rowing up the nearby River Rother to invade England. The king gave Sir Edward a "license to crenellate." (That meant he could build those towers that look like rooks in a chess game.) But to be a proper castle, Bodiam needed a moat.

THE STENCH OF DEFENSE

A moat's job was to keep intruders outside, where they belonged. Bodiam Castle's moat was very wide, thanks to a spring that flowed into it. But some say it was a washout. "There are no records of the castle ever having been attacked," says castle administrator, Cathy Roberts.

That may have been a good thing. Roberts says the moat would have been "so easy to drain that it would not have been any value as a defense." If anyone *had* drained the moat back then, they would have discovered what happens when thirty-three *garderobes* empty into a moat. What are those? Medieval toilets. Festering at the bottom of Bodiam's moat was three feet of silt, mud, and other (ahem) waste.

SECONDHAND MOAT

After Sir Dalyngrigge's bloodline died out, Lord George Nathaniel Curzon bought the castle. He drained the moat in 1925 to search through the muck for artifacts. Here are a few of the "treasures" he found:
- One half of an old handcuff
- One shoulder piece from a suit of armor
- One steel sword hilt
- One spearhead
- Two horseshoes (extra wide)

- Glass from the chapel window
- One bronze vessel (probably an incense burner)
- One iron circular frame (part of a fishing net)
- One iron door hook
- One black-glass wine flagon
- Three iron cannonballs
- Four stone catapult balls

QUACK ATTACK

When Lord Curzon died, he left all that he'd found to the people of England. (They must have been very grateful.) He also left them the castle, complete with moat. Today, the moat is full again. A large population of carp thrives in its waters. And there has finally been an invasion—a colony of ducks.

o o o

MORE MOAT-I-FACTS

A few more oddities found in castle moats.

- **Desmond Castle, Ireland:** a musician's lyre (a type of hand-held harp) made from the bone of *Cervus megaceros*, an extinct giant elk
- **Leeds Castle, England:** a warder's horn, which would have been used to announce arrivals at the gate
- **Tower of London, England:** the skulls of two lions and one leopard
- **Söder Castle, Germany:** 15 anti-vehicle mines placed there during World War II

THE SHOEMAKER AND THE ELVIS IMPERSONATORS

An Uncle John's Totally Twisted Tale

A POOR SHOEMAKER had only enough suede leather left for one pair of shoes. As he cut the shapes he needed, he accidentally spilled blueberry juice all over it.

"I am finished," he said. "I have no money to buy more suede." So he went to bed and cried himself to sleep.

In the morning, he found a pair of blue suede shoes on his worktable. He could not understand what had happened. *Did I make these in my sleep?* he wondered. The shoes were beautiful. Every stitch appeared to have been made by a master.

The front door opened, and a man with bushy sideburns and dark glasses rushed in. "I'm all shook up," he said. "I have a show tonight, and I can't find my shoes!"

"What kind of show?" asked the shoemaker.

But the man didn't answer. He'd spied the blue suede shoes and his eyes lit up. "How much?" he asked.

The shoemaker could see how excited the man was. He could also tell that the man must be wealthy, because he wore a shiny white suit dotted with jewels.

"One hundred dollars," said the shoemaker.

"Don't be cruel!" said the man. "How about fifty?"

The shoemaker thought it over. With fifty dollars he could buy leather for two more pairs of shoes. So he agreed.

"Thanks," said the man. "If you make more shoes like this, I'll send my show-biz friends over to buy them."

That evening, the shoemaker cut out suede for two pairs of shoes. He dyed it with blueberry juice. Then he went to bed while the suede dried. When he awoke, he was amazed to find two perfect pairs of shoes. Within minutes, he'd sold them to two other men who looked exactly like the man who'd bought the first pair, including the bushy sideburns.

The shoemaker bought more suede—enough for eight shoes. In the morning he found four pairs of blue suede shoes on his worktable. More bushy-sideburn guys in white bejeweled suits bought them.

"Tonight I will sit up and see who is doing this marvelous work," said the shoemaker. He hid in a dark corner of his workshop and waited.

At midnight, two tiny elves crawled in through a window. Their clothes were tattered and torn. They went straight to work with the blue suede, stitching, sewing, and hammering so neatly and quickly that the shoemaker could hardly believe his eyes. They worked until just before dawn, then they scampered away.

"Those poor little elves have saved my business," the shoemaker said to himself. "I will reward them with new clothes to replace the rags they've been wearing."

And what better outfits to make than shiny white suits dotted with jewels, just like the ones his new customers wore? He spent the day stitching the clothing, and in the evening he made tiny blue suede shoes. He set the presents on the table, and he hid again, eager to see the elves' delight.

When the elves arrived, they stared at the new clothing. "For us?" said one.

"Who else?" said the other.

They quickly undressed and put on the new outfits. "How do I look?" asked the first.

"Slick as a hound dog," said the second.

"No more Heartbreak Hotel for us," said the first elf.

The elves danced and wiggled their tiny hips and started to sing. "Let's run, run, run, run, runaway!"

"Wait!" The first elf stopped dancing. "What about the shoemaker?"

The shoemaker stood up from his hiding place. "Don't think twice." He waved a hand. "It's all right." So the elves clicked their blue suede heels and scampered out the window.

The shoemaker really didn't mind. He had missed making shoes. So he went back to work, and he prospered. On Friday nights, he visited the retro rock-and-roll club in town to watch the Elvis impersonators. His favorites were tiny compared to the others. But they looked great in their sparkly white suits and blue suede shoes.

THE END

Spot all the Elvis songs in this story? See page 286.

A VISIT TO THE WITCH DOCTOR

Just thinking about these weird cures might make you sick.

In the Zulu, Swazi, Xhosa, and Ndebele tribal traditions of South Africa, *sangoma* are healers who call upon dead ancestors to help diagnose and cure patients. Sangoma have a more familiar title: witch doctor. Tribal people swear by their witch doctors' skills. Most sangoma cures are made with ingredients such as plants. But cures like the ones below might be a bit harder to...swallow.

PROBLEM: Backache
CURE: Eat crocodile fat.

PROBLEM: You want to win a soccer game.
CURE: Eat lion fat.

PROBLEM: Your crops won't grow.
CURE: Bury a human skull in the field.

PROBLEM: You want to be elected President.
CURE: Eat a slice of brain.

PROBLEM: Stroke
CURE: Eat lizard flesh.

PROBLEM: You feel weak.
CURE: Eat ground-up finger bones.

PROBLEM: You're sleepy and low on energy.
CURE: Drink human blood.

PROBLEM: Your store needs more customers.
CURE: Bury a human hand under the entrance.

WIZARD HEADGEAR

If you make and wear this wizard hat, you will either gain massive magical power with no training at all... or become a stylish perch for birds and squirrels.

WHAT YOU NEED:
- Large sheet of construction paper
- Scissors
- Clear tape
- Quick-dry craft glue
- Twigs, acorns, leaves
- Old newspaper
- Silver glitter spray

WHAT TO DO:

1. Roll the construction paper to form a cone. Tape it in place and try the hat on for size. If it needs to be bigger or smaller, peel off the tape and adjust the size before taping it back in place.

2. Cut off the extra paper at the bottom of the cone so that the hat will stand up on a table.

3. On the next full moon (for extra power), go outside and gather twigs, acorns, and dried leaves.

4. Glue on these natural elements to decorate your hat. Let the glue dry for at least a few hours.

5. Set the hat on newspaper and spray it with glitter spray for that magical sparkly effect.

6. Put on your hat and feel the power of nature surging through your body (or those birds landing on your head).

THE THREE LITTLE JACKALOPES

An Uncle John's Totally Twisted Tale

ONCE UPON A TIME...there were three little jackalopes. They were homeless and sick of wandering the streets. So they decided to build houses. Because they had no money—and were big on recycling—they used building materials they found around town.

The first little jackalope took down all the old concert flyers he found stapled to telephone poles. He folded them into an origami house. It was as colorful as a rainbow, and he always had plenty of reading material.

Then one night, as the first little jackalope was reading his bathroom wall, a hungry Doberman came to his door. "Let me in!" he barked. "Or I'll huff and puff and blow your house down."

"I'm in the middle of something here," said the first little jackalope. "Come back later!"

The Doberman didn't want to come back later. He wanted jackalope for dinner. So he huffed and puffed and blew the origami house down. The first little jackalope pulled up his pants and ran as fast as he could to his brother's house next door.

The second little jackalope had built his house out of soda cans he found in the trash. The walls smelled as sweet as high fructose corn syrup, and when it rained, the cans made a pleasant tinkling sound.

Then one tinkly night, the same hungry Doberman dropped by. "Open the door!" he barked. "Or I'll huff and puff and blow your house down!"

The second little jackalope looked at his brother. "He's kidding, right?"

But the Doberman was not messing around. He huffed and puffed and blew the recycled-can house down. (This also made a pleasant tinkling sound, but the little jackalopes were too busy fleeing to care.)

The third little jackalope had built his house out of wads of ABC gum he'd found under park benches. He could stick anything to the walls of his house—bottle caps, seashells, his collection of Pez dispensers... He even stuck the toilet paper roll to the bathroom wall.

When the hungry Doberman came by, he tried his best to blow the gum house down. He huffed and puffed. Nothing happened. Then he coughed up the loogie stuck in his throat and huffed and puffed some more. Still nothing. So he walked up to the house and gave it a giant push. And...his paws stuck. He kicked the house. His foot stuck. Then he kicked the house with his other foot. (He was not the brightest bulb in the lamp.)

And that is how the three little jackalopes came to live in a very sturdy house with a scraggly Doberman stuck to it.

THE END

CONFUCIUS AND THE UNICORN

. . . .

You know those stories moms spread while bragging about their kids? This might be one of them. But we've mixed a lot of history with the myth.

COUGHING UP NEWS

Legend says that in 551 B.C., a young Chinese woman visited a holy shrine to pray for a son. As she prayed, a unicorn came to her and coughed up a tiny jade tablet. On the tablet was a prophecy: "You will give birth to a throneless king." What did that mean? Her son would not be a ruler, but he would be a great leader.

In Chinese mythology, dragons mark the birth of emperors. Unicorns mark the birth of sages (wise men). To thank the unicorn for the good news, the young woman tied a satin sash around its neck.

FOLLOW THE LEADER

As predicted, the woman gave birth to a son. His name: K'ung fu-tzu. (Westerners call him Confucius.) True to the unicorn's prediction, Confucius never served as a ruler of China. In fact, he thought the Chinese ruling class had a lot to learn. They lived in luxury and made commoners foot the bill. How? They forced their people to pay taxes…lots and lots of taxes.

Confucius believed that taking advantage of the

people was wrong. Rulers, he said, should lead by setting a good example. The people being ruled should support good leaders by being loyal followers.

JACK OF ALL TRADES

The history of Confucius is confusing. Why? Because there's a lot of fiction mixed in with the facts. Add in the many names the sage has been called, and the mix gets muddier: Kong Zi, Kong Fu-zi, Master Kong, Kong Qui, K'ung fu-tzi, and, more simply...The Master.

Before he became *The Master*, Confucius worked at odd jobs, such as accounting and caring for livestock. At age 50, he became a government official. First he was Minister of Public Works and then Minister of Crime. But before long, Confucius offended a duke—probably with his ideas about what makes a good leader. He was fired as a minister and sent into exile.

A LITTLE RESPECT

After that, Confucius became a traveling teacher. He spent his life creating a code of behavior based on the concept of *li*. *Li* means respecting others and performing rituals to create order and harmony. Here's an example: A friend comes by for a visit. To show respect, you treat the visit as a special occasion and offer your friend a cup of tea. In China, that doesn't mean plopping a tea bag into a cup and pouring boiling water over it. It means spending time to brew a perfect pot of tea (the ritual) and then serving it to your friend (the respect).

LIKE MOTHER, LIKE SON

When he was 70 years old, Confucius is said to have finally met his mother's unicorn. "In the spring," he wrote, "a unicorn was captured on an imperial hunt." Some versions of the legend say that the hunters had killed a strange beast in the woods. They had no idea what kind of animal it was, so they asked Confucius to take a look.

When he saw the animal, Confucius recognized it right away. How? The lifeless unicorn still had his mother's sash tied around its neck. Confucius had a good cry, and not just for the death of the unicorn. He believed the unicorn's end foretold his own death.

THE UNICORN'S LEGACY

Did the unicorn really exist? "The facts about Confucius are few and far between," says biographer Russell Freedman. "The spaces are filled in by legend and myth."

Those who study Chinese philosophy say that the unicorn represents good government. Confucius knew that the rulers of his day weren't ready for his ideas. He may have written about the unicorn to show that he feared his ideas would die with him. They did not. After his death, commoners and rulers alike began to follow the "Confucian Code." His ideas shaped Chinese government and society into the 20th century—that's about 2,500 years. Not bad for a "throneless king."

What did Confucius say—or not say? See pages 115–116.

TAKE THAT!

*The price of being royal in England? People make fun of you.
(Then again, if you want to keep your head...
hold your tongue.)*

KING HENRY VIII
"He was a blot of grease upon the history of England."
—**Charles Dickens, author**

QUEEN CAROLINE
"Most gracious queen, we thee implore, to go away and sin no more. But if the effort be too great, to go away, at any rate."
—**Anonymous**

KING CHARLES II
"Here lies our mutton-loving king, whose words no man relies on. Who never said a foolish thing, and never did a wise one."
—**John Wilmot, second Earl of Rochester**

QUEEN VICTORIA
"In heaven, she'll have to walk behind the angels—and she won't like that."
— **King Edward VII**

QUEEN CHARLOTTE
"I do think the bloom of her ugliness is wearing off."
—**Horace Walpole, author**

QUEEN ELIZABETH II
"She's just five feet, four inches tall. To make someone that height look regal is difficult."
—**Hardy Amies, designer**

PRINCE WILLIAM
"The prince isn't my type. He's too horsey-looking."
—**Keira Knightley, actress**

HOARD IT!
THE TOOTH FAIRY

. . . .

An Uncle John's Totally Twisted Tale

THE TOOTH FAIRY'S SON, BOB, could hardly believe it. His mother had been at it again. "Another tooth? Mother! Are you serious?" This time, television cameras were there to capture her obsession on film.

"It's special, son. Look…the cavity is shaped like a heart," said his mother. "And I have just the place for it." The tooth fairy flitted across the room and placed the tooth on top of a tiny red velvet cushion inside a lighted display cabinet. "Perfect!" She clapped.

"Mom, the house is already so full we can hardly walk," said Bob. "There are molars, incisors, baby teeth—even neonatal teeth. This has to stop. You have a serious problem. That's why the TV crew is here. This is an intervention."

"It's my job, honey. You know that," said the tooth fairy. "And what's that about TV?"

"Right there!" Bob waved his hands at the producer, the cameraman, and the sound specialist, a puzzled look on his face. How could she not have noticed them?

"Besides, your co-workers turn the teeth in at the dental repository. They don't take their work home," said

Bob. "For crying out loud, you're collecting from animals now! How many puppy teeth can one fairy gather?"

The tooth fairy looked at the carefully sorted teeth stacked around the room. "Really, son. It's not that bad," she said. "Besides, there are only a few specimens in your room. The fangs and the fossils."

"And that's another thing," said Bob. "Since when does the tooth fairy collect fossils? There are museums for those kinds of teeth."

"Museum!" She pressed her hands together and her wings started to glow. "Exactly. This is my tooth museum, and it's filled with treasures. Every tooth here is special to me. I couldn't possibly let any of them go."

"It's time for you to see the truth," Bob said, and he turned his mother to face the camera. "You're a hoarder. And the *Hoard It!* crew is here to help you see the truth."

"Son," the cameraman interrupted. "I don't know who you're talking to, but will this 'mother' of yours be here soon? We can't wait all day."

Bob glared at the cameraman. "She's standing right there. Are you blind?"

His mother took his arm and gave it a squeeze. "Don't be too hard on them. They can't see me."

"What! Why not?" Bob asked. "Because they don't believe in the tooth fairy?"

"Don't be silly." His mother smiled. "*Everyone* believes in the tooth fairy. But *I* don't believe in TV."

THE END

PLAY OGRE OBLIVION

....

Shooting spit wads at school: Bad idea.
Shooting spit wads to take out a team of ogres: Fun!

WHAT YOU NEED:
- Clean white paper
- Pen or pencil
- Large cardboard box
- Warm water (or spit)
- Scissors
- Clean drinking straws
- Tape
- Food coloring (optional)

WHAT TO DO:
1. Draw or trace ten three-inch ogre faces on white paper and cut them out. (Hint: Shrek heads work great!)
2. Tape the ogres to the side of a large cardboard box.
3. Prepare spit wads by tearing small pieces of clean paper into tiny strips, then soaking them in warm water (or spit—preferably your own).
4. When the papers are soaked, roll them into balls small enough to fit inside a drinking straw.

HOW TO PLAY:
1. Set the box about ten feet away from where you'll sit.
2. Place a spit wad in one end of a straw.
3. Forcefully blow the spit wad at the paper ogre faces. If the wads are juicy-wet, they'll stick.
4. Give yourself ten points for hitting an ogre square in the face, five points for hitting its outer edges, and

one point for hitting the box. If you miss the box, you lose a point. (And your parents may ground you. Ogre fighting is not without risk!)

5. If you're playing against another spit-wad sprayer, highest score wins each round. If you're playing alone, try to beat your own score on round two.

SPIT WAD FREE-FOR-ALL!

To make the contest between two ogre sprayers more exciting, add a different color of food coloring to the warm water each player uses to wet the spit wads. Now that you can tell which person shot each spit wad, have a free-for-all! Shoot at the same time rather than taking turns. May the best spit-wad warrior win!

o o o

OGRE JOKES

Q: Why don't ogres eat rich kids?

A: Because they're spoiled.

Q: Why did the dragon get fat?

A: Because it was an ogre-eater.

Q: Which beans do ogres like to munch?

A: Human beans.

Q: What's the difference between boogers and brussels sprouts?

A: Ogres won't eat brussels sprouts.

RIDICULOUS!

You should never feel silly using magic. At least, that's what the witch who shared these traditional spells told us.

- To prevent injuries, rub an onion on yourself and chant, "I am protected against all harm."
- Want to score at sports? Carry a bay leaf and picture yourself celebrating your big moment.
- To stop a dog from yapping, put leaves from the hound's-tongue plant inside your shoes. Then close your eyes and imagine a happy, quiet dog.
- For safe travels, pin a sprig of parsley to your shirt and picture a protective bubble surrounding you.
- Made someone angry? Write the person's name on a small piece of paper. Stick the paper in an ice-cube tray, pour water over it, and freeze it. Then imagine the person cooling off.
- To protect your money, picture blue flames bursting from the tip of your index finger. Use your flaming finger to draw a pentagram (five-pointed star) on your purse, wallet, or piggy bank.

MAGIC SPELLS are said to be based on three simple principles: **1.** Your thoughts create your reality; **2.** Your words create reality; and **3.** Your intentions create reality. So if you try any of these spells and something actually happens, you have only yourself to blame.

BRAZIL'S FOREST GUARDIANS

If you visit Brazil, be nice to the forest animals.
Otherwise, you might meet one of these guys.

RAINFOREST BOY

The Tupi people of Brazil tell of a strange boy who lives deep in the Amazon rainforest. His name is Curupira. He has blazing red hair and green teeth. His job: Protect wildlife from greedy hunters. If a hunter takes only enough game to feed his family, Curupira leaves him alone. But if a hunter shoots an animal for sport, not food? Watch out!

In the case of one greedy hunter, Curupira whistled shrilly so the hunter would follow his tracks. The hunter walked and walked, but he never caught up with the boy. Instead, he became hopelessly lost. Why couldn't he catch up? Curupira's feet point backward, so his tracks always lead *away* from him. The hunter never made it out of the forest. As for the deer he shot? The forest guardian whistled it back to life before going on his way.

THE FATHER OF THE FOREST

One day, legend says, a group of hunters was hot on the trail of some white-lipped peccaries. What they didn't know? The bristly pig-like peccary is a favorite animal of *Pai da Mata* (Father of the Forest). The hunters heard a strange whistle, but couldn't tell where it came from. Just then, a four-foot-tall black man with long shiny hair popped out from behind a tree! They had just enough time to notice that the little man was wearing a pair of shorts and nothing else, then *poof!* He vanished.

The peccary tracks they'd been following also disappeared, as if the trail had been wiped clean. With no trail to follow, the hunters got lost. They wandered around all day, and they didn't make it out of the forest until night fell. What did the hunters have to show for their perilous peccary hunt? Sore feet.

THE WOLF'S CAPE

Bullets can't harm him. His stench can knock a hunter right off his feet. And his howl? It freezes grown men in their tracks. The legendary *Capé Lobo* ("Wolf's Cape") is said to be an elderly Indian who left his village long ago to live alone in the forest. According to legend, a group of hunters once had their dogs follow a trail of fresh spoor (animal poop) into the forest. Suddenly, the dogs started to yelp. Something sounded very wrong.

When the hunters caught up, they found *Capé Lobo* flinging the dogs through the air. The hunters tried to stop him, but his smell was beyond horrible. They became so dizzy they could hardly stand. Somehow the sick hunters stumbled out of the forest and made it home…but the stench was so bad their stomachs churned for a whole month.

THE LEGEND OF BLUE BEARD

. . . .

An Uncle John's Totally Twisted Tale

ONCE THERE WAS A MAN whose beard was blue.
His name, fittingly, was Blue Beard. Blue Beard swore
that his bright blue facial hair was natural. He even
had a photo from his teen years that showed bulging
red zits poking through the sparse blue fuzz on his chin.
Embarrassing...but enough proof to secure his position
as head of the Pirate Guild of North Dakota. After
that, anyone who mentioned the words "hair dye" in his
presence disappeared without a trace.

It may be hard to believe, but despite his luxuriant
blue beard and important position, ladies weren't exactly
lining up for dates. Blue Beard blamed that on the fact
that he often had to travel on Pirate Guild business.

Still, one day, Blue Beard met the woman of his
dreams. Or so he thought. Unbeknownst to Blue Beard,
the woman was dating him for one reason: her sister
had vanished after going with him to see *Pirates of the
Caribbean*. And the lady was determined to find her.

One evening, Blue Beard invited the woman for
dinner. As she cut her Salisbury steak into bite-sized pieces,
she whispered to herself, "It's not real. It can't be real."

Now, Blue Beard had excellent hearing. "Of course

it's not real," he said. "It's a TV dinner."

"Right," she said. "The steak." She tried not to glance at his beard, but she couldn't help herself.

Blue Beard went eerily quiet and pushed his chair back from the table. "I must go away for a few days," he said. "To Bismarck. On Pirate Guild business. I wonder if you wouldn't mind watering my plants."

Perfect! The lady smiled. "Of course not," she said.

Blue Beard gave her his key ring. "There are plants in every room," he said, "except the cellar." He pointed to a tiny twisted key that unlocked the cellar door. "If you value our friendship, stay out of the cellar."

After Blue Beard left, the lady watered all of the plants. She found a pair of pruning shears among the kitchen tools and snipped off the dead leaves. Her promise kept, she headed straight for the cellar. When she opened the door, thousands of bottles of blue hair dye tumbled out, burying her up to her chin. "Help!" she cried.

"Sis?" A voice came from the back of the cellar. "Is that you?"

The lady's sister—and everyone else who had ever dared to suggest that Blue Beard dyed his beard—peered from behind the blue bottles. The butcher, the baker, the candlestick maker...they all blinked, but they did not move. "Hey!" the lady yelled. "I could use some help over here." None came to her aid. Not even her beloved sister.

They're ensorcelled! the lady realized. So she swam out of the bottles and waded to the cellar stairs.

When Blue Beard returned home, the lady was

sitting at the dining room table with an empty blue-dye bottle in her hand. "Hello, Blue Beard." She winked.

"You have betrayed me!" Blue Beard lunged across the table.

The lady brought the pruning shears from behind her back. "One more step and you'll be Blue Beardless!"

"No! Not the beard! Anything but the beard!"

The lady grabbed the villain by his blue beard and tugged him down to the cellar. She waved an arm at the people inside. "I'll keep your secret on two conditions," she said.

"Anything!" Blue Beard nodded.

"Good." The lady gave his beard a yank. Tears of pain welled up in his eyes. "First, release these people from your evil sorcery. And second, if you would keep your wretched beard, *they* must decide your punishment."

Blue Beard had no choice. He snapped his fingers and his victims slowly stretched themselves back to life. After a quick vote, his fate was sealed: He must dye his beard a new color—flaming orange.

Now, if you know your pirates, you'll know that there are plenty of Blackbeards and Bluebeards. But Orangebeards? Nary a one. The Pirate Guild stripped the villain formerly known as Blue Beard of his badge of office and booted him out the door. Last we heard he was working for the North Dakota Department of Transportation…as a traffic cone.

THE END

THE WHITE QUEEN'S RIDDLE

*Author Lewis Carroll, who wrote about Alice and
her adventures in Wonderland, was quite the riddler.
See if you can figure out the answer to this one.*

First pull up the fish,
It can't swim away: for a fish this is funny!
Next 'tis bought; and I wish
That a penny was always its adequate money.
Make it ready to eat—
Fetching pepper and vinegar won't take a minute.
Dish with cover complete,
Of lovely shell china, already 'tis in it.
Now 'tis time we should sup.
What's one only, you dolt? Set a score on the table!
Take the dish cover up—
With mere finger and thumb you will never be able.
Get an oyster-knife strong,
Insert it 'twixt cover and dish in the middle;
Then you shall before long
Un-dish-cover the Oysters—dishcover the riddle!

Answer to riddle on page 286.

SYLLABUBBLE, WITHOUT THE TROUBLE

*There's nothing like a good old-fashioned witches' brew.
But who wants to drink eye of newt and tail of slug?
Syllabub is just as bubbly, plus it's yummy and easy to make.*

WHAT YOU NEED:

SUPPLIES
- Drinking glass (or cauldron)
- Spoon

INGREDIENTS
- ½ cup apple cider or apple juice
- 2 teapoons sugar
- ¼ cup cream soda
- ½ cup whipped cream (or vanilla ice cream, softened)

WHAT TO DO:

1. Stir the apple juice and sugar together in your glass (or cauldron) until the sugar has completely dissolved.

2. Pour in the cream soda and stir once or twice more.

3. Top off the fizzy drink with a generous dollop of whipped cream or soft ice cream, and slowly stir the cream into the liquid. Don't worry if it starts to dissolve or curdle—that's part of the magic!

MUSICAL GHOSTS

Scotland has more than 1,000 castles. And some of their most famous residents can carry a wicked tune.

THE DRUMMER BOY haunts Edinburgh Castle. This headless ghost's drumming was heard for many years, but lately he's been seen—but not heard. Why? The drummer boy appears when the castle is under attack, and that hasn't happened since 1745.

THE PIANO PLAYER tickles the ivories in Castle Fraser. No one knows why the ghost plays. But some believe the piano player seranades a princess murdered long ago in the castle tower. Her body was dragged down the stone staircase leaving a bloody trail. No matter how many times the stains are scrubbed away, they always reappear. And so does the ghostly piano playing.

THE TRUMPETER has been blowing his horn outside Fyvie Castle since the 1700s. Locals say the player was a man who fell in love with the local miller's daughter. But the lord of the castle wanted her for himself. He sold his rival into slavery. By the time the man made it back to Scotland, the girl had died of a broken heart. On his deathbed, the man swore to return on the night before the death of every castle lord. He would blow a trumpet to remind everyone of the injustice he had suffered. And for many years, he…or someone…has.

THE PIPER of Culzean Castle is said to be an ancestor
of Scotland's Kennedy clan. Hundreds of years ago,
the castle's resident piper vanished while exploring the
caves below the castle. But that hasn't stopped him from
performing at family weddings. His ghostly bagpiping
floods the castle grounds every time a Kennedy marries.
    Because Scotland abounds with ghosts, you might
want to memorize this Scottish prayer before you visit:

> *From ghoulies and ghosties and long leggety beasties*
> *And things that go bump in the night*
> *Good Lord, deliver us!*

o o o

WEREWOLVES OF…SCOTLAND?
In the Highlands, ghosts may be the least of your worries.

PACKS OF MAN-EATING WOLVES once prowled the
Scottish Highlands. When their howls haunted the hills,
even the bravest men shivered in their kilts. Special safe
houses called *spittals* had to be built to protect travelers.
Scotland's wolves were so feared that by 1800 most had
been hunted down and killed. But one kind of wolf may
have survived. A family named Dickieson has an odd
carving on its coat of arms—a beast with a wolf's body,
long toes and tail, and a man's head. The beast was
known locally as the "war woolf." (*Aaa-hoo-oo!*)

THE FAIRY GAMEMASTER

An Uncle John's Totally Twisted Tale

NOT VERY LONG AGO...last week, in fact, there was a boy named Carl who lived with his very ancient and very scatterheaded great-aunt, Primrose Noodleman. All Great-Aunt Primrose ever did was take long Epsom-salt soaks in the tub with her rubber duckie and mumble about misplacing something important.

"It's your glasses, Aunt P.," Carl would say. "They're on top of your head." (They were always on top of her head.)

Carl didn't mind too much. He was old enough to take care of himself. But he wished he had someone around to challenge him on video games. He'd only asked Great-Aunt P. to play once. "Can't do it, kiddo!" She'd waved her gnarled fingers at him. "Arthur-i-tis. See?" Carl winced and stuffed his hands in his armpits. What if this Arthur-i-tis stuff was catching? That would be a major disaster.

You see, Carl was a gamer of some renown—a national champion, in fact. He had shattered all the high scores for his favorite game, *Blood-soaked Zombie Armies of Death.* Beating other players had become so easy that he played with all but one of his fingers taped together. Carl was getting a little desperate until one day (last week) he heard a knock at the door. Great-Aunt P. was playing with her rubber duckie in the tub, so Carl answered. A stooped little old man stood outside.

"Hello," he said. "Are you Carl?"

"Yes," said Carl.

"Splendid," said the man, and the bow tie he was wearing whirled like a pinwheel. "I am your fairy gamemaster."

"Right," said Carl, and he slammed the door and turned to head back to his room. "Crikes!" He braked so fast his sneakers squeaked. Just a foot away stood the elderly man, still smiling, his bow tie swirling to a stop. "H-how'd you get in here?" Carl stammered.

"Maybe you missed the 'fairy' part of my title?" The man wiggled his bushy white eyebrows. Then he clapped his hands. "Down to business. The video-game company sent me. No one is playing *Blood-soaked Zombie Armies of Death* anymore because everyone thinks it's impossible to beat your score. The company's losing money big time. So they hired me to beat you."

Carl snorted. The guy was ancient—at least 40. "So, kids who have been playing since they were toddlers can't beat me, and you can?"

The fairy gamemaster rubbed his veiny old-man's hands together and nodded.

"Fine." Carl invited the fairy gamemaster into the family room and turned on his game system. He picked up the tape to seal his fingers together, but the fairy gamemaster stopped him.

"Better not," he said. "You'll need all the help you can get."

Carl raised his eyebrows, but he didn't say anything. He just pushed *Start*, and then *Two Players*. Within a minute, sweat was dripping down Carl's forehead. He was ahead, but only by 10 points. And the fairy gamemaster had amassed the biggest army of blood-soaked zombies he'd ever gone up against. After another minute, the old man pulled ahead. Carl rubbed his sweaty forehead against his shoulder, not daring to stop toggling for even a second. He couldn't remember the last time he'd had so much fun.

Ten seconds later, the first round was over. The fairy gamemaster had wiped out Carl's zombies with a laser lobotomy ray. Carl hadn't even known the game *had* a lobotomy ray! The next round was even worse. With a hip twist that looked like it could break a bone, the FGM shot a bright green fart-bomb out of a zombie's backside. Carl's zombies turned into green sludge, and the fairy gamemaster's zombies danced around in a blood-soaked zombie frenzy. The FGM's score rolled higher and higher and higher until...*Kaboom!* The TV exploded.

Great-Aunt Primrose ran into the living room, tying on her robe. "What was that?" she yelped.

The fairy gamemaster dropped his controller. "Primrose?" He took one of Great-Aunt P.'s gnarled hands in his and brought it to his lips.

"Ew!" Carl shut his eyes.

"My darling! Is this where you've been for the last two years?" asked the FGM.

Great-Aunt Primrose blinked. "Where are my glasses?" she asked. "Has anyone seen my glasses?"

"On your head, darling!" The fairy gamemaster eased the glasses down onto her nose. She blinked a few more times, and then her mouth fell open.

"Noodleman? Is that you?"

"Huh?" Carl looked from the fairy gamemaster to his great-aunt and back again.

The next day, Bow Tie Noodleman—the great-uncle his great-aunt had misplaced—showed up with all his stuff, including a trunk filled with more gaming gear than Carl had ever seen.

Carl was in gamer heaven. He had a zombie-killing gamemaster living right in his house. And Great-Uncle Bow Tie had promised to take him on as an apprentice. "But you're going to have to practice more than you have been." He winked. "If you want to earn your wings."

THE END

o o o

"The only time I worry about the press is when I'm up at Balmoral fishing. When I'm standing in the river for hours, I sometimes have a pee in the water. I'm petrified some cameraman is going to catch me at it."

—**Prince Charles of England**

sOCCER SORCERY

Winning at soccer requires strength, teamwork, and speed.
(But a little magic doesn't hurt!)

HUDDLE BEFUDDLE

Most sports teams rely on coaches to pep up players for a win. Some African soccer teams have a different strategy: They hire witch doctors to "bend the lines, bewitch the ball, befuddle the referees, and paralyze goal keepers," says African journalist Bartholomäus Grill.

The use of *juju* (magic) to change a game's outcome is so common that fans watch for hexes and spells as closely as they watch the match. During one pro game in Kenya, a dog wandered onto the playing field, lifted its leg, and peed. The fans went wild. They were sure someone was using the dog as juju to win the game.

SKIPPY AND THE JUJU

During soccer season Jackson Ambani is a busy man. The hand-lettered sign tacked to his shack on the outskirts of Nairobi, Kenya, reads, "Witch doctor." Ambani has practiced juju in East Africa for more than 40 years. "Juju works," he insists.

Ambani works juju for several Kenyan soccer clubs. Before a game, he rubs a "secret green powder" on his hands. (Sorry. He won't reveal the ingredients.) Then he dumps seashells out of a Skippy peanut butter jar. The

shells show him whether his client's team would win
without his help. If not, the witch doctor goes to work.

First, he tosses a bit of cloth clipped from an
opposing player's clothes into a clay pot. Then he adds
herbs. He learned the best ones to use from his juju
elders. (Don't ask…they're secret.) Next he puts in blood
from chickens and porcupines. The juju Ambani brews is
meant to "trip up" the player during the match and help
his client's team win.

GOALS AND GORE

Ambani isn't the only witch doctor working for soccer
teams. It's not unusual to see a witch doctor smearing
pigeon's blood around an opposing team's locker room
before a game or sprinkling the ashes of dead animals
near the other team's goal. One witch doctor even tried
to bury a live cow in front of the other team's goal to
guarantee a win. (Officials stopped him.)

Juju isn't free. Ambani charges from $20 to $2,000,
depending on how much magic a team needs. According
to one source, "Some teams spend so much money on
juju, they can't afford to travel to away games." And if
a client doesn't pay up? The witch doctor works magic
against the client's team.

REVENGE OF THE WITCH DOCTOR

In 1992, the Ministry of Sport for the Ivory Coast
hired witch doctors to help the country's team—the
Elephants—win the Africa Cup. The Elephants did

win: 11 to 10. But the Ministry didn't pay the witch doctors. Bad decision: the witch doctors cursed the national team. The Elephants fell into a slump that lasted ten years. In 2002, the Minister apologized to the witch doctor and paid the $2,000 still owed.

NO CANNIBALS ALLOWED!
Former soccer player Roger Milla says it takes more than magic to make a winning team. He thinks his country, Cameroon, proves it. "We are not strong in witchcraft," Milla said. "But our football is better than in those nations where magic is so strong."

Milla isn't the only one trying to downplay the role magic plays in African soccer. The Confederation of African Football (CAF) has been trying to stop soccer juju for years. "We are no more willing to see witch doctors on the field than cannibals at the concession stand," the CAF official said.

DO YOU BELIEVE?
It's as tough to stop soccer magic in Africa as it would be to make Africans quit playing—and loving—the game. From Algeria to South Africa, and in just about every country in between, entire nations grind to a halt when a big game of "football" (their name for soccer) is on TV.

For those who would rather practice juju than attend soccer practice, *Botswana Sports Magazine* printed this warning: "There is no evidence that football games can be won through witchcraft alone."

FAIRY SURPRISES

Things you may not know about world-famous fairies.

ARIEL
First Appeared to Humans: 1611, in William Shakespeare's play *The Tempest*.
Known For: Summoning storms (tempests), causing shipwrecks, and helping people fall in love. Before that, Ariel spent 12 years stuck in the hollow of a tree, thanks to an evil witch.
Surprise! Ariel is a *boy*, not a girl. But female actors played the part of Ariel from the mid-1600s until 1930.

THE BLUE FAIRY
First Appeared to Humans: 1883, in Carlo Collodi's *The Adventures of Pinocchio*.
Known For: Helping Pinocchio transform from a puppet to a real boy. The Blue Fairy also makes Pinocchio's nose grow…and grow…and grow whenever he lies.
The Surprise: She can turn herself into a blue mountain goat. (How cool is that?)

THE SUGAR PLUM FAIRY
First Appeared to Humans: In 1892, in a ballet called *The Nutcracker* by Pyotr Tchaikovsky.
Known For: Wearing ballet slippers and performing "The Dance of the Sugar Plum Fairy." The fairy's dance

has become a popular Christmas treat all over the world.
Surprise! The Sugar Plum Fairy's first performance,
(in St. Petersburg, Russia) was a flop. Critics called her
"corpulent" and "podgy"—fancy words for "fat."

TINKER BELL
First Appeared to Humans: 1904, in J.M. Barrie's play,
Peter Pan.
Known For: Speaking fairy language (which sounds like
golden bells tinkling) and leaving fairy dust on the hands
of anyone who carries her.
Surprise! Tink is the jealous type. If Peter Pan pays
attention to other females—especially the human girl,
Wendy—watch out! Once, in a jealous rage, she told the
Lost Boys to *shoot* Wendy with their bows and arrows.

THE COTTINGLEY FAIRIES
First Appeared to Humans: 1917 in Cottingley, Britain.
Known For: Showing up in photos. Fifteen-year-old Elsie
Wright and her ten-year-old cousin Frances Griffiths
took the photos. Sir Arthur Conan Doyle—who wrote
the Sherlock Holmes mysteries—believed the girls when
they said the fairies were real. He even wrote an article
called "The Evidence for Fairies" for a magazine.
Surprise! When Frances and Elsie were elderly women
(in the 1980s), they admitted that the fairies in four
of the photos were made using hatpins and cardboard
cutouts. But the *fifth* fairy photo? They swore that one
was real.

THE FART KING

An Uncle John's Totally Twisted Tale

IN THE REDWOOD KINGDOM of the Far West lived
an aging mountain lion. He had been king of the forest
for many years. He was a kind and fair-minded leader,
and the other animals respected him. But his strength
had faded, and he knew that he would soon die. He
gathered the animals around him and told them that it
was time to choose a new king.

"I am strongest," said the bear. "I should lead."

"But I am wisest," said the owl. "I would be the best
king."

"I am both strong and wise," said the elk. "I should
be in charge of the forest."

The skunk pushed his way to the front of the
crowd. "Only one animal can make you all run in fear,
and that is me," said the skunk. He raised his tail, and
the bear, the owl, and the elk scrambled backward.

The skunk did not spray. He laughed. "My scent
is more powerful than *all* of you. Unless any of you can
match the power of my smell, the throne belongs to me!"

Little Rabbit hid beneath the ferns nearby,
listening. He was so frightened by the bigger animals
that he farted.

"Ugh!" said a squirrel. "That smells awful."

"Worse than awful," said a chipmunk.

Little Rabbit had an idea. *If I'm that smelly, maybe I could be king,* he thought. *Imagine that! A little rabbit like me, king of the forest!*

Little Rabbit hopped to the front of the gathering. "I challenge you to a fart contest," he said to the skunk. "The winner will be king."

Little Rabbit bent forward, raising his tail. He farted long and loud. The animals scurried away.

"Ha!" said the skunk. "Your fart smell lasts for only a few seconds. My odor can last for days." And he lifted his tail and sprayed the poor rabbit.

Little Rabbit fled home to his burrow. When he got there, the other rabbits would not let him in. "You smell like Skunk," they said. "Come back when you are odor-free."

That night, Little Rabbit nearly froze to death hiding among the forest ferns. It was many days before he was allowed back into the rabbit burrow. In the meantime, Skunk took the throne as king of the forest, threatening to spray anyone who challenged his rule.

All of the animals lived in fear. They couldn't stand the new king, but anyone who protested was sprayed. Soon, the entire forest smelled of skunk spray.

"We must do something!" said the squirrel.

"But what?" asked the deer. "The skunk is powerful. If we protest, he will spray us again."

The animals secretly made their way to the den of the former king. The mountain lion was weak and near death, but he let them in.

"Oh, kind king," said the raccoon. "Our new leader is a tyrant!"

The lion raised one feeble paw. "The solution is in all of you," he said. "No one creature can match the strength of dozens." And then the lion closed his eyes... and died.

"What did he mean?" asked the mole. "The skunk has the most powerful odor of all. How can we overpower him?"

Little Rabbit was so excited that he farted again. The others backed away, and suddenly the rabbit knew what to do. "None of our farts alone are a match for the skunk's odor," he said. "We must all fart together! Together, we can destroy him!"

"To the bean patch!" trumpeted the elk.

"To the bean patch!" echoed the owl.

The animals ate their fill of ripe, juicy beans. Then they waited for digestion to begin.

"I feel something gurgling," said the deer.

"Yes," said the bear. "The time to strike is at hand."

The animals crept through the forest. They found Skunk napping on the throne, and they formed a circle around him. And then...they fired! *Ptt-oo-oo-t-t-t!* The sound of farts filled the air.

Gas hit the skunk from every angle, overpowering him with its stench. He jumped off the throne and ran as fast as he could to get away from the terrible smell. And he was never heard from again.

The animals decided to form a three-creature panel

to rule the forest. The owl, the bear, and the elk were elected.

As for Little Rabbit, he was given a medal—for extreme bravery under fire.

Moral: Many small farts can bring down a tyrant.

THE END

o o o

FUN FACTS ABOUT FARTS

o Termites produce more farts for their size than any other creature. Because they mostly eat wood, they need lots of bacteria in their guts to help digest it. Bacteria produce a lot of gas, so the termites fart repeatedly to release it.

o For some time, scientists have said that cow farts play a role in global warming. Now they're saying it's not cow farts; it's cow *burps*. Cow farts stink, but they don't have a lot of methane in them. Because methane holds onto a lot of heat when it gets into Earth's atmosphere, it is the gas that contributes most to global warming. Cow burps are full of the stuff. And just one cow can burp up 243 pounds of methane a year.

o How much power is in a fart? If you could fart without stopping for six years and nine months, it would equal the explosive energy of a nuclear bomb.

FWUMP

How did you get so smart?

I'm a wandering wise man.

It's in the job description.

Geez, I guess the tower didn't come with shampoo.

Rapunzel?

I'm afraid not.

Rapunzel's tower is 4 score and 7 blocks south.

I'm Abe Lincoln.

Do you happen to have a spare razor?

HA! CRAVEN KNIGHT!

. . . .

Before journeying to the realm of castles and kings, you'd better brush up on your Olde English insults.

INSULT: "Pah! Hast thou no kissing-comfits?"
MEANS: "Yuck! You need a breath mint."

INSULT: "Thou art a blathering fiddlehead!"
MEANS: "Your head is as empty as a fiddle and you talk too much."

INSULT: "This grub tastes like one."
MEANS: "This food tastes like maggots." (Back then, it actually might have been.)

INSULT: "Open your wink-a-peeps, you whifling zuche!"
MEANS: "Open your eyes, you insignificant tree stump!"

INSULT: "Barlafumble, whilst thou art still able!"
MEANS: "Give up while you can!"

INSULT: "Away with yon snawky slibber-sauce!"
MEANS: "I am not taking that nauseating medicine."

INSULT: "What a poop-noddy thou art!"
MEANS: Either "You're a dummy" or "You're making a fool of yourself for love."

INSULT: "Thou art prone to pumpkinification."
MEANS: "You are so full of yourself."

INSULT: "Whiteliver!"
MEANS: "Coward!"

HOW TO MAKE A WISH

Ever heard the story about the kid who ate so many Pop Rocks his stomach exploded? Actually, that's a myth, but you get the point: Be careful what you wish for!

WHAT YOU NEED:
- Large bowl
- Rice paper
- Scissors
- Tea candle

WHAT TO DO:
1. Fill a large bowl with warm water.
2. Cut a one-inch square of rice paper.
3. Write a word on the square to symbolize your wish.
4. Drop the square into the water.
5. Ask an adult to light the tea candle. (Yes. An adult. Burning down the house is not considered lucky.) Float the lighted candle on the water.
6. As the candle burns, picture holding what you wish for in your hands. Don't blow out the candle. Let it burn until it goes out on its own.
7. Once the candle burns out, dig a hole, pour the water and the paper into the hole, and cover them.
8. Keep picturing your wish coming true.

K-9ery Row

An Uncle John's Totally Twisted Tale

TIMES WERE TOUGH on K-9ery Row. The dog-food cannery had closed, so the dogs were out of work. They hung around the boarded-up cannery all day, watching the ocean as it crashed on the rocks below the pier.

Like most of the unemployed dogs, a mutt named Lucky ate his meager meals at the soup kitchen. Then he wandered over to the pier and curled up, hoping his grumbling belly wouldn't keep him awake all night.

One evening, on the way to the pier, Lucky ran into his friend Snarl. "Those pinch-penny Poodles at the soup kitchen don't give us enough to stay skinny on," Lucky complained. "I'm still starving."

Snarl picked some gristle out of his teeth with a toenail, and then wiped his graying muzzle clean on his matted coat. "Be thankful for what you get," Snarl said.

"Thankful?" Lucky snorted. "For the trash they feed us? Tastes like ground-up cat guts. I'd rather eat maggots."

"Here," Snarl said. He pushed his last scrap of food toward Lucky. Lucky ate it without a word of thanks.

The next morning, Lucky got up early to beat the rest of the starving mutts to the garbage cans. Every can had already been picked clean. So Lucky headed along the empty road. Months before, trucks had filled the

road, coming and going as they picked up loads of dog food from the cannery. Now the road was empty.

Lucky kept walking until he caught a whiff of something wonderfully fishy and rotten. And it was close by! Lucky bounded up a small slope and was thrilled to find a dead salmon. Had it fallen off a truck before the cannery closed? He poked the fish with his nose. It still had plenty of oozing flesh. Yum! Lucky nudged aside some flies and picked up the fish with his teeth, maggots and all.

Lucky glanced around and spotted Snarl coming up the road. His friend looked thin and hungry. *Sorry, buddy,* Lucky thought as he trotted away. *This fish isn't big enough for the both of us.*

Lucky cut through the back alleys of K-9ery Row and headed toward the pier to eat his catch. He went all the way to the end. Before he sat down, he glanced into the water and spotted…another dog! And that dog had a tasty, rotten salmon, too!

I should take that fish, Lucky thought. *I'll save it for tomorrow.*

Lucky leaned over the edge of the pier and opened his mouth wide to snatch the other dog's fish. When he did, his own salmon fell into the water with a plop. Lucky yelped. *My fish!* But when he reached down to retrieve it, a giant mouth filled with razor-sharp teeth thrust toward him.

No…it wasn't Lucky's reflection. The mouth belonged to a great white shark. Lucky pulled back, but he was too late. The shark swallowed him in one gulp.

A few minutes later, Snarl wandered along the tide line sniffing for food. The tide was going out. Just beyond the breakers, he saw a huge fin break the water's surface, and then disappear.

Snarl padded on. Pretty soon he came to a dead salmon washed up beneath the pier. Snarl grabbed the prize and trotted happily back toward K-9ery Row. *This fish is big enough to share,* he thought. *I wonder where my friend Lucky is right now?*

Moral: *A fish in the mouth is better than being in the mouth of a fish.*

THE END

o   o   o

WHAT'S SO FUNNY?

THERE ONCE WAS A DOGLIKE BEAST with a smile that stretched from ear to ear. It was said to have lived around two thousand years ago, in India and Ethiopia. It's name: the *crocotta*. Some say the crocotta hunted people. It tricked its prey into coming into the woods. Then it would attack. Why would anyone be fooled? The crocotta could imitate the sound of someone calling for help. Long thought to be a creature of legend, scientists now think the crocotta was actually an ancient hyena.

REAL-LIFE PRINCESSES

*Here's proof that the life of a princess isn't
all tiaras, balls, and Prince Charming.*

o As a child, England's queen, Elizabeth II, was known
as PRINCESS LILIBET. As a teen, she had a few
flirtations, just like most young women. One was with
Prince Philip of Greece. How did her parents react?
Her mother thought Prince Philip would make a fine
match, but her father disagreed. "His wardrobe is
ghastly!" said the king.

o PRINCESS STéPHANIE of Monaco earned the
nickname "wild child" in her teens. Why? She has at
least seven tattoos, including a flower chain around
her wrist and a snaky dragon on her back. "I may be a
princess," she said, "but above all, I'm a human being."

o As a little girl, PRINCESS CHARLENE wasn't scared
of anything. "Once she jumped off a tree onto a horse
and broke her arm in three places," her father said.
She's a vegetarian who eats lots of garlic and chili,
and she's also a South African swimming champion.
Charlene has something in common with the classic
fairy tale princess, Cinderella. What? She wasn't born

a princess. She married a prince—Princess Stéphanie's brother, Prince Albert II of Monaco.

○ What would it be like to grow up in a palace? According to PRINCESS HAYA of Jordan, "When the doors were closed, it was a home. There was laughter and water fights!" But when she asked her father, the king, for a horse, he hesitated. Jordan is a conservative country. What would people think of a princess on horseback? "Daddy, every princess has a scandal," Princess Haya reminded him. The king bought the horse, and Haya named it *Scandal*.

○ Women are not allowed to drive in Saudi Arabia. They have to rely on male relatives to drive them, or hire male drivers. PRINCESS AMIRA AL-TAWEEL is hoping for change. She gets behind the wheel whenever she can. "I have an international driver's license," Amira says. "And I drive in all the countries I travel to."

○ PRINCESS BEATRICE of York is most famous for... a hat. At the wedding of her cousin, England's Prince William, Beatrice wore a tan hat that made her look as if she had a giant pretzel perched on her head. The thing was a foot tall. The hat got so much buzz, it ended up with its own Facebook page. "It has its own personality," says Beatrice. What did the princess do with the hat after the wedding? She auctioned it off and raised $130,000 to support two children's charities.

BAG OF RUNES

Runes are ancient symbols that can be used to predict the future. Here's a way to bake your own set.

WHAT YOU NEED:
- Small package of white polymer clay
- Toothpick
- Baking pan
- Aluminum foil
- Acrylic paint (optional)
- Zipper-lock or drawstring bag

WHAT TO DO:
1. Decide how many runes you'd like to make. Form a ½-inch clay ball for each rune. Flatten each ball by pressing on it with your thumb.

2. Use a toothpick to carve a rune symbol into each clay rune. (Choose from the symbols on pages 251–252, but leave one rune blank.) Carefully scrape off any bits of clay left sticking up after carving the rune.

3. Preheat your oven to 275 degrees. Line a baking pan with a sheet of aluminum foil. Place your clay pieces, rune-side up, on the foil. With an adult's help, put the runes into the oven. Bake them for about 30 minutes, and let them cool for at least that long.

4. (Optional) For colored runes, paint them with acrylic paint and let them dry completely before storing.

5. Store your runes in a zipper-lock or drawstring bag. *Ready to predict the future? Turn to page 250.*

o o o

MAKE MINE MEAD

Ever wonder why some people are poets? Our favorite explanation comes from the Vikings.

Viking myth has two races of gods: the Aesir and the Vanir. As gods tend to do in mythology, the two races went to war. At the war's end, the gods decided they would all spit in a jar to seal the peace. They used the spit to make a man who was sent into the world to spread wisdom. Some wicked dwarfs killed the man and mixed his blood with honey to make a magical mead. (Mead is a potent drink, usually made from fermented honey and water.) The dwarfs called their potion "The Mead of Poetry."

Some time later, the dwarfs handed over the mead to a powerful giant to keep him from squashing them to jelly. The giant hid the mead in a cave. Odin, top god of the Aesir, heard that the giant had the Mead of Poetry and went to find it. When he did, he gulped down the entire vat, turned himself into an eagle, and flew back to Asgard (home of the gods). Most of the magic mead made it back to the gods, but Odin spilled a little during his flight. It fell to Midgard (Earth), and that is why humans can become poets.

TURN LEAD INTO GOLD!

According to modern science it can't be done…
but that hasn't stopped people from trying.

SCIENCE, MADNESS, OR MAGIC?

In the Middle Ages (roughly A.D. 400–1600), men of
"science" spent a great deal of time trying to turn
metals like lead into gold. Sound nutty? Maybe not.
One of the most famous scientists of all time tried
for years.

Remember Sir Isaac Newton, the scientist who
liked to watch apples fall to the ground? Those apples
helped Newton figure out how gravity works. But he also
spent a lot of time at a furnace, brewing foul-smelling
mixtures of mercury, lead, sulfur, and other ingredients
in a quest to turn them into gold.

PRESTO, CHANGE-O!

The art of turning one thing into another (like cheap
metals into valuable ones such as gold) is called *alchemy*.
The practice thrived in Europe during the Middle Ages.
But it was illegal. Kings feared that alchemists really
would make gold. If they did, that extra gold could ruin
a country's monetary system. (Of course, many of those
same rulers ordered alchemists to try to make gold. Why?
To swell the royal treasuries.)

RECIPES FOR FAILURE?

In their attempts to make gold, alchemists concocted *elixirs*. Elixirs might include anything from plants to metals, eggs, or even human hair. After mixing an elixir, the alchemist added it to a common metal and then heated it. Most alchemists kept their recipes secret. Newton wrote his recipes in riddles like this one:

> *This is the magic fire of the wise to heat the King's bath*
> *(which within a week's prepared).*
> *Unlock it which thou mayest do in an hour,*
> *and after wash it with a silver shower.*

Fortunately, some alchemists used plainer words. Here's a recipe for making gold bracelets: "Take two parts lead and one part gold, and grind the metals into fine powder. Mix the powder with gum." (Not chewing gum. Probably *gum Arabic*, which comes from the sap of the acacia tree.) "Use the sticky mixture to coat a ring of cheap metal, such as copper. Heat the metal ring. The mix will harden and look like pure gold." The problem: The copper ring doesn't really turn into solid gold. It just looks like gold.

Our favorite recipe promised to turn donkey urine into gemstones. For those who happen to have donkey pee on hand, here's what to do: "Take white lead, one part, and of any glass you choose, two parts, fuse together in a crucible, and then pour the mixture." Next, add "the urine of an ass." Wait about 40 days, and the mixture will turn into emeralds.

A HISTORY MYSTERY

Why would a scientist like Sir Isaac Newton waste his time on alchemy? "It was perfectly reasonable for Isaac Newton to believe in alchemy," says Dr. Bill Newman, a history of science professor at Indiana University. "Most of the experimental scientists of the seventeenth century did."

Alchemists might not have made gold, but they created all kinds of useful compounds. They gave artists better paints, sick people new drugs, and smelly people stronger soaps. *Transmutation*—breaking down one compound and turning it into something else—is still an important part of the scientific process. It's used to make everything from ink to gunpowder to cosmetics. No one has turned lead into gold (yet), but alchemists like Sir Isaac Newton laid the groundwork for a modern field of science: *chemistry*.

THE SECRET BEHIND THE SECRET ART

Of course, alchemy didn't start with Isaac Newton. A clue to its origins is hidden in its name. *Alchemy* comes from the Arabic word *al-Khem*, which means "from the Land of Khem." And *khem* is the Egyptian word for the rich black soil of the Nile River delta. Alchemy is rooted in the "secret arts" of ancient Egypt.

By 3000 B.C. Egyptians are thought to have already mastered many processes related to working with metals and chemicals. The penalty for sharing those secrets with outsiders was death. So how did their secrets spread?

When Alexander the Great conquered Egypt and became Pharaoh (332 B.C.), he stole the scrolls filled with Egypt's secret knowledge and had them translated into Greek.

That still leaves a big question: How did the Egyptians master metallurgy and chemistry thousands of years ago? Egyptian myth says that "god-like" beings came "through the Void" and settled in Egypt. These beings taught mankind "all the secrets of nature," including the art of alchemy. Were they gods…or aliens? We may never know.

TWO MASTERS OF ALCHEMY

o **JABIR IBN HAYYAN** (circa A.D. 721–815) This Arabian alchemist wrote down his formulas in a language he made up. Why? At the time, alchemists were thought to be sorcerers. The penalty for sorcery was death. So Jabir didn't want anyone else reading what he'd written. The modern word *gibberish* (nonsense) came from his name.

o **ROGER BACON** (circa A.D. 1214–1292) According to the Bible, humans once lived to be 900 years old. This English scientist wanted to create an elixir that would let people live that long again. Did he succeed? Hard to say. When Bacon claimed the ancients lived longer because they were more moral than Christians, monks nailed his books to library shelves and let them rot.

FAIRY-TALE TONGUE TWISTERS

Before you try these tongue twisters, you may need to sprinkle fairy dust on your tongue.

To start a fairy flying fast
fly faster than the flying fairy starts.

Which witch switched wands?

Starry elves stuck in the star thistle.

Pour a cup of coffee from a copper coffeepot.

Crabby king crabby king crabby king.

When snow blows the knight knows to blow his nose.

Six shiny stars show signs of shining.

Tales dragons tell smell.

Prince Zith's sister plays a zither.

Tommy the tuba tooter tutored two tooters to toot.

Ugly ducklings don't dunk doughnuts.

SOCKED IN

An Uncle John's Totally Twisted Tale

MAYDAY! MAYDAY! Sixteen-year-old Miles stared
at the instrument panel in his Cessna cockpit. The
gauges were spinning out of control. He had no idea of
the plane's altitude, air speed, or direction. One minute
he'd been flying along the Florida coast without a cloud
in the sky. The next, he was flying blind inside a cloud
bank black as the inside of a clothes dryer.

Miles reached into the glove box to get his maps.
He peered at the area closest to where he'd been when
his instruments went berserk. "Oh, no," Miles whispered.
"The Bermuda Triangle."

The Triangle was legendary. In 1910, a Navy ship
vanished with 309 sailors aboard. Five bomber planes
went missing in 1945. Yachts, airliners, tankers—all
kinds of vessels had disappeared in the triangle of ocean
between Florida, Bermuda, and Puerto Rico. There were
plenty of theories: magnetism, pirates, tropical storms,
dimensional portals, even aliens had been blamed. Was
Miles about to discover the mysterious triangle's secret?

The aircraft began to shudder. Miles fought to keep
the throttle engaged, but failed. The airplane started to
dive, nose first. He had only seconds before gravity would
decide his fate. He reached down between his knees
and grabbed the handle of his ejection seat. *Wham!*

The canopy separated and Miles was blasted into the air along with his seat. Wind sucked at his cheeks, and rain scoured his skin. Then his parachute opened and jerked him away from the falling aircraft.

Miles took a deep breath, and for just a moment he thought everything might be okay. Then lightning crackled across the sky, and his nylon chute went up in flames. Miles plummeted. He wished he'd given his mother one more hug. He wished he'd played fetch one more time with his bulldog, Chomsky. Most of all, he wished he'd taken more flying lessons before going solo. Miles closed his eyes and braced for impact. Then he hit: *FWUMP!*

Fwump? Not *sploosh* or *splat* or *crunch?* Miles fumbled in the darkness trying to figure out what had broken his fall. His hands touched something soft and lumpy. Clouds? *That's it,* Miles thought. *I'm dead. And this is heaven.* Then he sniffed. Heaven smelled familiar. Flowery. Like the dryer sheets his mom used.

As the clouds cleared, Miles looked around, ready for his first glimpse of the afterlife. And he saw...socks! Millions and zillions of socks. Tube socks. Argyle socks. Crew socks. Socks with little yellow duckies. An ocean of socks had broken his fall. And not one of them had a match. Miles had found the solution to two of the world's biggest mysteries: missing socks and the Bermuda Triangle. As for whether he ever found his way home... that's another story.

THE END

THE MAGIC TEAKETTLE

Rumor has it, Grandma Uncle John got this magic tea recipe from her fairy godmother. Brew a cup to see if the magic works for you!

WHAT YOU NEED:

SUPPLIES
- Teakettle
- Mug
- Tea ball
- Spoon
- Airtight container

INGREDIENTS (For 16 servings)
- ½ cup of loose orange or lemon tea
- 5 rounded tablespoons of berry rooibos tea
- Honey

WHAT TO DO:

1. Mix the two types of tea together and store them in the airtight container.

2. To make one cup, heat enough water in the kettle to fill your mug.

3. While the water warms, scoop 2 teaspoons of magic mix into your tea ball and close the ball tightly.

4. When the teakettle sings, turn off the heat and carefully pour the hot water into your mug.

5. Stir ½ tablespoon of honey into the hot water, set the tea ball into your mug, and allow the mixture to steep for five minutes.

6. When the time's up, take out the tea ball and sip up the magic!

THE REAL MAGIC: Nutritionists say citrus teas (like orange or lemon) contain enzymes that keep your immune system strong and your brain on high alert. Adding rooibos to the mix has a soothing effect. And honey is rich in vitamins and minerals that our bodies need for health. Science or magic? You decide.

o o o

CHINA'S FIRST TEAPOT

Here's what happens when royalty boils water.

One windy day in 2737 B.C.—so the legend says— Emperor Shen Nung was outside boiling water. A few green leaves blew into the pot. Shen Nung wasn't about to stick his royal hand into the boiling water and pull them out, so he waited. Pretty soon, the brew began to smell yummy. So Shen Nung decided to try a cup.

Luckily, the leaves came from a shrub called *Camellia sinensis*, and they were perfect for making tea. They're still used today to make green tea, oolong tea, and black tea. So why was an emperor boiling his own water? We have no idea. But it makes a great story!

VANISHING CLOAK

Want an invisibility cloak like Harry Potter's? Read on.

BELIEVE IT OR NOT, scientists have been working on making things invisible for years. Now, researchers at the University of Birmingham (England) have taken what they say is a giant step. They have discovered that a crystal called *calcite* is great at bending light.

What does bending light have to do with invisibility? "The way we see is basically light being reflected off of objects," said Jacob Ward, editor of *Popular Science* magazine. When light bends, the eye can be fooled into seeing something that's not there—or *not* seeing something that *is* there.

On a hot sunny day, drivers often see what looks like a puddle shimmering in the road up ahead. But the splash never comes. Why not? That puddle isn't water. It's a mirage made by heat bending rays of light.

Something similar happened when scientists placed calcite over a paper clip. *Zing!* The paper clip seemed to disappear. A paper clip may be a lot smaller than Harry Potter, but it's thousands of times bigger than anything scientists have made "vanish" before.

Calcite crystals can be up to 21 feet long. In theory they could make a kid who wants to skulk around school invisible. But there's still a problem to be worked out: the "cloak" itself—for now just a calcite block—is visible.

DRAGON SIGHTINGS

Think dragons disappeared long ago?
Here are three that may still be lurking around.

ICE-SEE A DRAGON

Since 1345, stories have spread about a massive creature living in Iceland's Lake *Lagarfljót*. The 25-mile-long lake is 367 feet deep in places. That means it's dark and icy enough to hide a water dragon. In 1987, witnesses saw the *Lagarfljótsormurinn (Lagarfljót Worm)* curled up in an inlet near a campsite. In 1998, a teacher and a group of students spotted the lake dragon near the shore. They said it looked like a huge worm. Then in 2012, grainy footage of the creature showed up on YouTube.

Some people thought Iceland's water dragon had finally been captured on video. But Loren Coleman, director of the International Cryptozoology Museum in Portland, Maine, disagreed: "The Icelandic lake monster has been described as a pale, humped animal, about fifty feet long, sprouting whiskers on the head at the end of a six-foot-long neck." To Coleman, the creature in the video looked like a robot made with fish nets and trash bags. In other words, this sighting, at least, could be a hoax.

QUARRY SPOTTED

In 2001, a British natural history expert claimed to have seen a snake-like dragon flying over a quarry in Powys,

Wales. The creature had four short legs and a head that looked like a sea horse. It flew in a wide circle. Was it searching for something? Looking for prey?

"It was neither an optical illusion nor a model, but was truly alive," said the naturalist. As he watched the "dragon" soar over the quarry, a chill washed over him. The creature was green and its skin shimmered. He watched for several minutes until the beast vanished into what looked like a crevice in the wall of the quarry.

"I had the distinct impression that this creature was deliberately warning me off from approaching its territory," said the naturalist. He heeded the warning.

MONSTER ALERT

In 2011, kayakers on England's Lake Windermere said they saw a dragon swimming in the lake. It had three or four humps and swam very quickly.

"At first I thought it was a dog," said kayaker Tom Pickles. "But then I saw it was much bigger. Each hump was moving in a rippling motion, and it was swimming fast. Its skin was like a seal's, but its shape was completely abnormal—not like any animal I've ever seen before."

The kayakers took a photograph, but the shot turned out blurry. It's hard to tell how big the creature is, though it looks like it could be eight feet long or more. There appear to be humps and what might be a head. Sound familiar? Perhaps the kayakers saw a cousin of Scotland's legendary Loch Ness Monster. But for now, the encounter is being reported as a dragon sighting.

DISAPPEARING FAIRY FINGER PUPPETS

Turn your fingers into fairy puppets. And when you're done, eat them! (The puppets, not your fingers.)

WHAT YOU NEED:
- Nontoxic markers
- Honey
- Colored sugar crystals
- Fruit leather
- Marshmallows
- Knife (and a parent's help so your fingers stay attached)

WHAT TO DO:
1. Draw a fairy face on the fleshy part of your first finger (the opposite side from the nail).
2. Wrap a fruit leather "dress" around your finger.
3. Spread honey on your fingertip and sprinkle on colored sugar crystals to make sparkling fairy hair.
4. Cut a thin round slice from the top of a marshmallow. Cut the marshmallow circle in half. Use honey to stick the two halves to your finger to make fluffy fairy wings.
5. Now let your fairy finger act out your favorite fairy tale—any tale will do.
6. When you're done, make your fairy "disappear" by gobbling up the evidence.

*Want more fairies? Dress up more fingers,
or invite your friends to join the fun.*

STINKING BEAUTY

....

An Uncle John's Totally Twisted Tale

PRINCE CHARMING was kind of a big deal. By the time he was nineteen, he'd slain seven ogres, defeated a giant, vanquished two dark sorcerers, and won four chili cook-offs with his own secret recipe. Now he was bored.

"Two hundred gold pieces to the first one to bring me a quest worthy of my many talents," he declared.

Before long, a line stretched around the castle.

"There's a fair maiden held prisoner in a far-off tower," said a knight. "If you can climb the tower and rescue her, she'll…"

"Fair maidens are a dime a dozen." The prince yawned. "NEXT!"

"I know of a magical sword encased in stone," said a young page. "Whoever can remove it shall be king."

"My kingdom already awaits," said the prince.

"Mind if I have a go, then?" asked the boy.

"Knock yourself out," said the prince. "NEXT!"

"A giant lives at the top of this tall, tall beanstalk in our garden," said a farmwife. "He has a golden goo—"

The prince cut her off. "Please. Do I look like I need more gold?" He waved a hand at the two hundred gold pieces awaiting the winner of the challenge. "Has no one a quest of true worth and daring?"

Just then a stranger came forward. "I have a quest,

mate," he said in a strange accent. "A right perilsome venture what might save a princess and her whole bloomin' family from a cursed castle."

The prince leaned forward. "Go on," he said.

"She's been sleepin' fer a hundred years, she has, in a castle what's choked by deadly thorn vines and guarded by a galloping-big dragon. You'll have to fight your way through both thorns and dragon, see? Then wake up the fair maiden wiff a kiss."

"Hmmmm…," the prince murmured. "These vines. Just how deadly are they?"

The stranger chuckled. "Ask the bones of those who've gone before you. There are dozens of skeletons tangled in them vines."

"And the dragon?"

"Huge. Foul. Starvin', mate."

"And the princess?"

"Beautiful beyond compare. But there's one thing about her you should know—"

"Enough!" the prince cried. "I accept the challenge!"

And so Prince Charming set out on his journey that same day and soon arrived at the castle. The thorny vines, though quite thorny indeed, yielded to his blade, and he hacked his way past the bones of the losers who'd gone before him. The dragon was tough, but the prince was tougher. By noon he was flossing his teeth with its sinews. *I should have gone with the beanstalk*, he thought.

Then he opened the door to the sleeping princess's bedroom and spotted…a real beauty.

"Wow! She's HOT!" Prince Charming hurried across the room and knelt beside the princess's bed. But just as he leaned in to kiss her rose-red lips, she let out the smallest of sighs. Her breath blew Prince Charming backward. He slammed against the castle wall.

"HOLY SMOKES!" The prince gagged. "That's the worst thing I've ever smelled." Brave though he was, Prince Charming could not bring himself to make a second attempt. He fled from the castle with a cry of defeat on his lips: "*Stinkus breathus vincit omnia!*" (Stinky breath conquers all.)

THE END

o o o

PRINCE CHARMING'S LATIN LESSON

Match the Latin phrase with its English translation—because you never know when a little Latin will come in handy.

1. *Dum vivimus servimus.*
2. *Ad astra per alas porci.*
3. *Draco dormiens nunquam titillandus.*
4. *Ex luna scientia.*
5. *Hic sunt leones.*
6. *Cave, vomiturus sum!*

a. Look out! I'm going to barf.
b. While we live, we serve.
c. To the stars on the wings of a pig.
d. From the moon, knowledge.
e. Never tickle a sleeping dragon.
f. Here there be lions.

Answers on page 286.

THE WANDMAKER'S WORKSHOP

Why wait for the wand to choose the wizard? Make your own!

WHAT YOU NEED:

- Wand-sized stick (collected beneath a full moon if possible)
- Gold, silver, or black spray paint (for light or dark wizardry)
- Newspaper
- Glitter glue
- Unsuspecting parent
- Glue gun
- Magic talisman (such as a marble, crystal, feather, or shell)

WHAT TO DO:

1. The perfect stick for a wand must be as long as the distance between your elbow and wrist. It should be dry, sturdy, and free of sharp bumps or splinters.
2. Place your wand on the newspaper. Spray-paint one side. When that side dries, turn the wand over and paint the other side. Let it dry again.
3. Decorate the wand with glitter glue. Let it dry, and then turn the wand over. Decorate the other side.
4. Find an unsuspecting parent with a glue gun. Ask the parent to glue your talisman onto the wand.
5. When the glue dries, use your wand to make the parent forget the whole thing.

CONFUCIUS SAID

Did someone follow the ancient Chinese philosopher Confucius around writing down every word he said? He didn't say. But here are a few things he did say.

"Never give a sword to a man who can't dance."

"No matter how busy you may think you are, you must find time for reading, or surrender yourself to self-chosen ignorance."

"Have no friends not equal to yourself."

"If you see what is right and fail to act on it, you lack courage."

"A lion chased me up a tree, and I greatly enjoyed the view from the top."

"When you have faults, do not fear to abandon them."

"The superior man loves excellence: the petty man, his own comfort."

"If there be harmony in the home, there will be order in the nation."

"What you know, you know. What you don't know, you don't know. This is true wisdom."

"To study and not think is a waste. To think and not study is dangerous."

CONFUCIUS: "I prefer not speaking."
STUDENT: "If you do not speak, what will we have to record?"

CONFUCIUS DIDN'T SAY

The real Confucius wasn't a comedian—he was a thoughtful man who said wise things. So all those jokes that begin with "Confucius say"...Not Confucius.

Confucius didn't say: "A dog who runs behind a car gets exhausted."

Confucius didn't say: "A boy who sneezes without a tissue takes matters into his own hands."

Confucius didn't say: "He who eats too many prunes sits on toilet many moons."

Confucius didn't say: "If you live in a glass house change in the basement."

Confucius didn't say: "A man who crosses the ocean twice without washing is a dirty double-crosser."

Confucius didn't say: "He who keeps both feet firmly planted on the ground will have trouble putting on his pants."

Confucius didn't say: "A house without a toilet is uncanny."

Confucius didn't say: "She who eats crackers in bed wakes up feeling crummy."

Confucius didn't say: "He who farts in church must sit in pew."

Confucius didn't say: "Time flies like an arrow. Fruit flies like bananas."

OUTFOXED!

················

An Uncle John's Totally Twisted Tale

THERE ONCE WAS A MAN with two sons who were twice as dumb as they were lazy. "You boys need to start pulling your weight," he told them. "If you want lunch today, you're going to have to chop some firewood."

Ralph and Alf headed toward the forest with a saw and an axe. They were hungry, so they stopped at Aesop's Takeout Stand for a sack of burgers and fries. Just as they started to eat, they spotted their father's pickup truck headed toward them. So they stashed their lunch in a hollow tree and hurried into the woods.

When they were out of sight, a greedy fox climbed into the tree and started gobbling down the fast food. He ate four hamburgers and two stupor-sized orders of fries. Then he licked his lips and tried to climb out of the hole. He couldn't. His stomach was bloated to twice its normal size. The fox began to whine.

Another fox heard him crying. "You're trapped because of your own greed," she said. "And you'll be stuck there until you've grown thin again."

But the trapped fox was clever. He figured he could outsmart the boys and get away safely. He climbed into the empty lunch sack. The boys would have to widen the hole to get it out.

When the boys got back to the tree, they were

hungrier than ever. Ralph reached for the sack. "I can't get it out," he said. "It's too big!"

"Don't be dumb," said Alf. "We put it in there. We can get it out."

Ralph pulled, but the sack wouldn't fit through the hole. "Maybe the food swelled up when it got cold," he said, wiping his nose on his sleeve.

"You're right," said Alf. "Cold makes things swell up something awful."

The fox chuckled. Now the boys would have to cut a wider hole. In a matter of minutes, he'd be free.

"You know, now that those burgers are cold, they'll be disgusting," said Alf.

"And the fries will be mushy," Ralph said.

"Paw promised us lunch for cutting wood," said Alf.

"Yep," said Ralph.

So they left the firewood where they'd stacked it and started walking home.

The fox was stunned. It looked like he'd have to wait until he was thinner, after all.

Halfway home, Alf turned to Ralph. "I've been thinking," Alf said. "We can't leave that food in the tree to rot. Some poor animal might eat it and get sick."

So Ralph found a board to seal the hole in the tree. And Alf hammered it into place. "That's better!" they said, and they hurried home to lunch.

Moral: Outsmarting dumb people is harder than you think.

THE END

KING ARTHUR'S MYSTICAL ISLE

. . . .

*Could the legendary island called Avalon
exist in the real world?*

CLAIM TO FAME

The town of Glastonbury in the United Kingdom claims
a connection to the legend of King Arthur. The town
council says that a nearby hill is the site of Avalon,
the mystical island on which Arthur and his queen,
Guinevere, lived, died, and were buried.

The hill is called Glastonbury Tor. *Tor* is the
Middle English word for a bare or rocky hill. Glastonbury
Tor looks unnatural, artificial, as if raised by men (or
magic). It can be seen from twenty miles away, sticking
up above a flat green landscape. The remains of a
pathway thousands of years old spiral up the hill.

But there's one big problem with Glastonbury Tor
being the site of Avalon: It's a *hill*, not an island.

WHERE'S THE WATER?

Things change, says the town council. "It is believed
that originally the settlement did lie among lakes and
marshland." That appears to be true. The area is not far
from the sea, and at the end of the last ice age, about
12,000 years ago, melting ice flooded the low-lying plain.
For thousands of years, several feet of water covered the

area. It's possible that the Tor was still surrounded by water in Arthur's time (said to be around A.D. 500).

ARTHUR GETS TREED

In 1191, the town's link to King Arthur was strengthened by a discovery at Glastonbury Abbey. Monks there claimed to have found the burial site of Arthur and Guinevere. Inside a hollowed tree trunk (some say an oak coffin) they found the body of a huge man.

"He was probably slain by a sword wound to the head," the monks said. Beside the man's bones were the smaller bones of a woman, with golden hair still stuck to her skull. When monks touched the hair…it turned to dust. The monks also found a lead cross inscribed with the words, "Here lies buried King Arthur, in the Isle of Avalon."

THE HOLE IN THE STORY

Was the body really King Arthur's? Hard to say. In 1278 the remains were transferred to a black marble tomb and moved to the Abbey Church. In 1539, vandals broke into the abbey and carted away all the valuables they could find…including, it seems, the bodies.

There are many legends about King Arthur's life and death, but little proof to back them up. However, in 1962 archaeologists dug where the monks claimed to have found his grave. They unearthed a pit, about five feet across, exactly where the monks said they had found Arthur's and Guinevere's remains.

COCKROACH AND THE HOUSEHOLD PESTS

THE HOUSEHOLD PESTS HAD BEEN TOGETHER FOR YEARS. MOUSE AND CRICKET DREAMED OF STAGES AND SPOTLIGHTS. BUT BRIGHT LIGHTS SENT COCKROACH SCUTTLING INTO THE SHADOWS.

SO THEY SPENT THEIR NIGHTS JAMMING ON A STREET CORNER. UNTIL ONE EVENING...

PSST!

COME WITH ME AND I'LL MAKE YOU A STAR.

HEY? WHERE'S MOUSE?

PROBABLY POWDERING HER NOSE. AGAIN....

BY JOHN O'BRIEN

COLOR POWER

Watch out! The color you wear may change your day.

RIDE THE WAVELENGTH. Light can be tricky. Take sunlight—it may look white, but it contains a rainbow of colors. And each color has its own wavelength. A rainbow shows off the wavelengths visible to the human eye: *red, orange, yellow, green, blue, indigo,* and *violet.*

Because color is made of up light, the body soaks it in, mostly through the eyes and skin. Every single cell in the body uses light energy. That's why color therapists claim that color can affect our bodies and our emotions.

Some scientists call color therapists "crackpots," but 1,500 hospitals and correctional institutions across America now have bubble-gum-pink walls. Why? Because officials are convinced that pink can keep patients (and inmates) calm. So choosing your clothes based on how colors affect you might be worth a try!

WEAR BLUE FOR A CALMER YOU. Blue is the coolest color, so it might help you keep your cool when dealing with difficult people (like that kid shooting spit wads on the school bus). To really relax, wear blue and imagine yourself floating in blue water.

GET AHEAD. WEAR RED. Even if the other team is undefeated, wear red if you want to win the big game.

Red is the color of blood, passion, and power. And it projects confidence. If your team jersey isn't red, wear red underwear and let the power of red soak into your skin.

HAPPY FELLOWS WEAR YELLOW. Next time you feel down, pick up your mood by wearing yellow. This color is also all about looking on the sunny side of life.

CHANGE THINGS. WEAR GREEN. Green—as in growing plants—is all about making things new. It's also the color of hope. When you're ready to change something in your life, change into green clothes.

DON'T BE BORING! WEAR ORANGE. Tired of being ignored? Put some orange in your life. It's the "fun and flamboyant" color, and it attracts attention. Orange is also warm, so it could be the key to making new friends.

KICK BACK! WEAR BLACK. Black absorbs instead of reflecting light. Wear black if you want to hide from unwanted attention (although you may attract vampires).

WANT PIZZAZZ? GO PURPLE. Red excites and blue calms. When you mix the two colors, you get purple. So wearing purple may make you feel a bit…unbalanced. But purple is the perfect color for days when you want to be creative: It inspires art, music, and poetry. And if you want to feel regal? Pull out those purple socks. Purple has been the color of royalty for thousands of years.

BEASTLY ORIGINS

. . . .

*Ever wonder if mythical beasts were based on something
real? Here's what scientists and historians think.*

THE BEAST: Centaur

THE MYTH: Half-man, half-horse, centaurs are wise,
fierce, and really skilled with a bow and arrow.

THE THEORY: Centaurs weren't beasts at all. They were
horseback riders. From a distance, someone riding a horse
would look a lot like a beast—half-man and half-horse.

THE FACTS: One archaeologist calls horseback riding
"our first form of rapid transit," but where and when did
people first saddle up? Historians aren't positive, but the
first horsemen may have been from a tribe called the
Botai. They lived in the vast grasslands between Central
Asia and Europe about 5,500 years ago. Mounds of horse
bones have been found in pits where the Botai once
lived. Some of the teeth show wear patterns that could
have been made by a bit in the horse's mouth. If so, that
could mean the horses were being bridled and ridden.

THE BEAST: Mermaid

THE MYTH: Half-woman, half-fish, mermaids swim
in waters all around the world. They're often seen
staring into mirrors and combing their long hair
(which is sometimes green). They have bewitching
voices, and they use them to lure sailors to their deaths.

THE THEORY: People didn't see mermaids; they saw manatees—big gray aquatic mammals with paddle-shaped tails and two front flippers.

THE FACTS: Tales of mermaids were familiar to explorers like Christopher Columbus. He wasn't surprised when he spotted three of them off the coast of Haiti in 1493. What did surprise him? They were "not as pretty as they are depicted, for somehow in the face they look like men." If the theory is correct, Columbus spotted *manatees*, and they have wrinkled faces and whiskers on their snouts. (Talk about manly!)

THE BEAST: Griffin
THE MYTH: Griffins are four-legged beasts with the head, beak, and talons of an eagle and the body of a lion. Griffins can fly. So they live in nests high up in mountains. Their job? To guard gold and other priceless treasures.

THE THEORY: Descriptions of griffins were based on the fossilized bones of a dinosaur called *Protoceratops* (pro-toe-SAIR-uh-tops).

THE FACTS: More than two thousand years ago, miners dug for gold in parts of Asia's Gobi Desert. They found huge beaked skulls sticking out of hillsides, and the bones of four-legged beasts scattered in the sand. When miners saw these bones, they pictured creatures with body parts like those of animals they had seen: eagles and lions. But the fossils belonged to *Protoceratops*, a dinosaur that lived from 86 to 71 million years ago. It had four legs, as a lion has, and a beak, like an eagle has. But it didn't have wings. The dinosaur's long shoulder blades may have made people think the creature had wings.

THE BEAST: Cyclops
THE MYTH: These huge human-like creatures had just one enormous eye, right in the middle of their foreheads. They worked as blacksmiths, doing especially fine work for the Greek gods. For Zeus, father of gods and men, they made a thunderbolt. For Poseidon, the sea god, they made a trident. And for Hades, lord of the underworld, they made an invisibility helmet.
THE THEORY: The giant beast with one huge eye was an elephant.
THE FACTS: In A.D. 400, a Greek philosopher named Empedocles wrote about giant fossil skulls found in caves along the coast of Sicily. He believed the skulls could be those of the race of giants known as *Cyclops*. Others agreed. What made them think so? The large central hole where the elephant's trunk would have been looks like an enormous single eye socket.

o o o

MR. WIZARD: Did you put the cat out?
MRS. WITCH: I didn't know it was burning.

THE LOCH NESS PRANKSTER

. . . .

An Uncle John's Totally Twisted Tale

THE LOCH NESS MONSTER and her buddy the giant eel were hiding behind a boulder at the edge of the lake, watching a motorboat tug through the icy fog.

"Watch this!" Nessie nudged her friend.

"Don't do it," Squirt begged.

"They want to see a monster," said Nessie. "We can't disappoint them."

"Sure we can," said Squirt. "They'll put you in a net and carry you away. Then who will I hang out with?"

"Don't worry, Squirt," said Nessie. "They're humans. They can't tell a monster from, I don't know, a hollow log. Watch!"

Squirt's mouth gaped open as Nessie launched a hollow log across the lake, straight toward the noisy boat.

"Careful," Squirt whimpered. "They'll see you."

"See me?" Nessie chuckled. "Not with those cameras pressed to their noses. Hey!" Nessie glanced at Squirt. "Did the water just get warmer?"

Squirt blushed. "I only peed a little. And it's your fault. You know what happens when I get scared!"

The log drifted through the water toward the boat.

"It does sort of look like you," Squirt admitted.

The log seemed to have a long neck, a horse-like head, and a thick-barreled middle. Four branches broke the lake's surface just where Nessie's fins might be.

"I see it!" hollered a chubby lady in an orange life jacket. "Just like the monster I saw last year. Get closer!"

The people on the boat stood up and pointed, rocking the boat sideways.

"Steady!" said the driver. "You'll swamp the boat."

A balding fellow wearing a bow tie and a houndstooth jacket stared into a video camera and started talking. "The monster measures about thirty feet long. And look how it paddles? Such graceful strokes."

"Is that video camera working?" demanded a man in a wet suit. "Hand it over and I'll swim closer."

Just then the drifting log sank into the depths of the frosty water.

"Nessie has bested us again," said the man in the bow tie. "It's almost as if she's playing tricks on us." Then he shook his head. "Sorry. That's no way for a scientist to talk."

Nessie nudged Squirt. "Want to give it a go? You could pretend to be me!"

"Don't be silly." Squirt wriggled. "Even humans aren't dumb enough to mistake a giant eel for the Loch Ness Monster."

THE END

TREATS TO CATCH A LEPRECHAUN

Most people think it takes gold to catch a leprechaun. But Uncle John found a tasty alternative: green cookies! (Caution: the smell of cookies baking may attract humans, too.)

WHAT YOU NEED:

SUPPLIES
- Bowl
- Whisk
- Spatula
- Plastic wrap
- Baking sheet

INGREDIENTS
- 3 tablespoons sugar
- 2 tablespoons butter, softened
- ½ egg, beaten
- ⅓ cup smooth peanut butter
- Green food coloring
- ⅓ cup flour
- ⅛ teaspoon baking soda
- ⅛ teaspoon salt

WHAT TO DO:

1. Put the sugar, butter, egg, peanut butter, and a few drops of green food coloring into the bowl. Whisk them all together.
2. Use the spatula to mix in the flour, baking soda, salt, and sugar. Stir until the batter is smooth.
3. Wrap the dough in plastic wrap, and put it in the

refrigerator to chill for half an hour.

4. While the dough chills, preheat the oven to 325 degrees. Take out the dough and pinch it into six or eight balls of equal size.

5. Roll each ball in your palms, flatten the balls slightly, and place them on your baking sheet.

6. Bake the cookies for about 12 minutes and then let them cool.

7. Place the cookies on a plate and let the leprechaun catching begin!

o o o

LUCKY CHARMS
Tips to keep the little people from playing tricks on you.

o Wear your coat inside out.

o Leave a tiny honey cake or some doughnut holes on your windowsill.

o Stick a sprig of holly in your hair.

o Use chalk to draw a pig's head on your door.

o Keep an acorn in your pocket.

o Always leave a single sock under your bed.

o Carry an anchor—or, if that's too heavy, put an anchor charm on a chain or bracelet.

o Find a wren's feather and keep it with you.

o Hang a pair of fuzzy dice from your bicycle handlebar.

o Wear a bell to chase away tricksters (although…you might be mistaken for a cow).

Inspired by Mother Goose

Three Silly Huntsmen

by Valeri Gorbachev

One day, the three silly huntsmen went fishing.

I think we'll catch the big one today.

FAIRY-DUST WISHES

Make bottles filled with fairy dust and good wishes!

WHAT YOU NEED:

- Newspaper
- Small bottles with lids or cork stoppers
- A small funnel (a cake-decorating nozzle works well)
- Assorted colors of glitter
- Dried crushed red, yellow, or orange flower petals
- Dried crushed lavender
- Small, blank stick-on labels

WHAT TO DO:

1. Wishes are the most important part of fairy dust. Choose a good wish for yourself or for the person to whom you'll give the fairy dust.

2. To make your fairy dust, you'll need a flat working surface out of the wind. Cover the surface with newspaper.

3. Use flower petals or lavender, depending on the wish. Lavender is calming. Use that for soothing wishes. Flower petals have sunny colors. Use petals for more intense wishes.

4. While thinking of your wish, use the funnel to pour your choice of petals or lavender into the bottle. Pour enough to form a shallow layer.

5. Next, add a layer of glitter. Choose cool colors such as

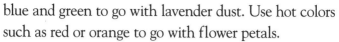

blue and green to go with lavender dust. Use hot colors such as red or orange to go with flower petals.

6. Alternate layers of glitter and lavender, or glitter and petals, until the bottle is filled.

7. Label the bottle with your wish, for example, *Good Luck, Sweet Dreams,* or *First Kiss.*

8. If the fairy dust is a gift, add a note that says, "To activate your wish, sprinkle a bit of fairy dust beneath your bed." *Then let the magic happen!*

o o o

ABRACA...HUH?

Remember—magic words work best when spoken aloud.

o "Klaatu. Barada. Nikto."
—from the movie The Day the Earth Stood Still, 1951

o "Hooey fooey chop suey gefilte fish!"
—professional magician Tom Kovnats

o "Bats in the belfry, pigs in a poke. Lose this bunny before I choke."
—from the 1960s' TV series Bewitched

o "Boomerang, toomerang, soomerang."
—from Mister Rogers' Neighborhood

o "Arzemy barzemy yangelo igg lom...abra cadabra!"
—from The Merlin Effect by T.A. Barron

o "Owa tagu siam!"
—comic magician, the Amazing Gregory

THE WOLF GIRL

An Uncle John's Totally Twisted Tale

THERE ONCE WAS A GIRL with long black hair that
fell to her waist in glossy strands. All the girls in school
envied her. And all the boys wanted to sit behind her in
class so they could practice tying her hair into the knots
they were learning in Boy Scouts.

The girl with the beautiful hair had a huge
crush on a werewolf boy. When the moon was full, she
followed him around like a sick puppy. But he always
ditched her and ran off with his pack. The girl knew he
wouldn't hang out with her unless she did something
drastic. So she paid a visit to the town witch. The witch
offered a trade: she would turn the girl into a werewolf in
exchange for her long glossy hair.

"Okay," said the girl, who was tired of brushing
her hair a hundred strokes every night to make it shine.
(Not to mention getting it caught in the revolving doors
at the mall.)

The witch waved her hand, and—*Poof!* The girl
was bald. "Nice doing business with you," said the witch.

"Is that it?" asked the girl. "Am I a werewolf?"

The witch smirked. "Wait for the next full moon,
girlie. You'll see how a witch keeps her word."

The girl bought an entire collection of cute hats to
cover her baldness. "Not bad!" she said, admiring herself

in the mirror. As she counted down the days until the next full moon, she imagined what it would be like to nuzzle snouts with the werewolf boy.

When dusk fell on the night of the full moon, the girl went outside. She sat in the darkness, shivering a little as she waited for the moon to rise. As it did, she began to feel strange. Her bones creaked and stretched. Her nose grew longer and wider (and became wetter and colder). Her knuckles gnarled and her fingernails curved into claws. Then her thoughts changed from words and pictures into swirling clouds. She gave a great sniff, threw her head back, and howled.

With her transformation complete, the wolf girl trotted over to the lair where her werewolf crush hung out. Doing her best to impress, she leaped right into the middle of the pack. Then, just to make sure the werewolf boy noticed her, she howled long and loud. A few seconds passed in total silence. Then the werewolves started snorting and howling and rolling on the ground like a pack of laughing hyenas.

What was wrong? Why wasn't the werewolf boy nuzzling her snout? A gust of wind whirled through the lair, and the wolf girl shivered. That's when it hit her. She was *freezing*. And a wolf—covered in fur—would not feel cold. She wasn't just a bald girl with a collection of cute hats, she was a hairless werewolf. And that, my friends, is how a witch keeps her word.

THE END

WITCHES' BREWS

Double, double toil and trouble;
Fire burn and cauldron bubble!

YUM'S (NOT) THE WORD

The "double trouble" line above is pretty famous. It was
written by William Shakespeare, an English playwright
during the late 1500s to the early 1600s. In the play
Macbeth, Shakespeare has three witches cook up an evil
potion with these repulsive ingredients:

> *fillet of a fenny snake*
> > *eye of newt*
> > > *toe of frog*
> > > > *wool of bat*
> > > > > *tongue of dog*

What really went into that cauldron? In
Shakespeare's time, many people believed that women
who were skilled with using plants to cure diseases were
witches. And most of the horrible-sounding ingredients
in their potions came straight out of the garden.

WITCH PLANTS

- **Fillet of a Fenny Snake**
  The Fens is an area along England's North Sea. It
  was swampy and marshy in Shakespeare's time, and it
  most likely did have snakes. But "fenny snake" was the
  nickname for one type of lily.

- **Eye of Newt**

  Some witches might have extracted the eyeballs from amphibians, but "eye of newt" was a flowering herb, also called *wild mustard*. It was said to aid in "traveling by air" (Maybe they *were* witches!) and to protect against cold, and colds!

- **Toe of Frog**

  Believe it or not, frogs do have toes. But this ingredient probably referred to the nickname of a flower: the buttercup.

- **Wool of Bat**

  One species of woolly bat can emit a sound every five milliseconds. That makes it one of the world's fastest "talkers." Why couldn't it talk its way out of a witch's brew? It didn't have to. "Bat's wool" was another name for moss.

- **Tongue of Dog**

  Witches *are* rumored to be cat people, but don't worry: "Hound's tongue" is a weed with leaves shaped like a dog's tongue. Witches used it to cast spells that would force others to keep silent.

BREWING UP TROUBLE

Of course, some brews called for ingredients that are just as horrible as they sound. Some witches believed the plants in their potions would be stronger if they added the blood, bone, or skin of an animal. So bear claws, cat

ears, mole teeth, or mice bones might be tossed into the pot. And some of the most powerful potions even called for human blood and flesh.

To make a truly evil potion, a witch would spit on the young seedlings. When the seedlings grew, the witch would harvest the plants beneath a full moon. And then she had to find her way home with a torch held in the hand of a corpse.

DOUBLY TROUBLING

If witches were really just healers who used herbs with creepy names, why were they so feared? In Shakespeare's day, horrible things happened that no one could explain. The worst: A plague called the Black Death swept through England and killed more than 80,000 people. Londoners were terrified, and the Globe Theatre where Shakespeare's plays were performed was shut down.

The plague was actually caused by bacteria, and the disease was passed from person to person by fleas. Since no one knew that at the time, they blamed "witches."

o o o

QUEEN ELIZABETH I ruled England during Shakespeare's time. In 1562, she passed a law titled *An Act Against Conjurations, Enchantments and Witchcrafts.* The law said that anyone who used "Witchcraft, Enchantment, Charm, or Sorcery, whereby any person shall happen to be killed or destroyed" was to be put to death. Witchcraft remained a crime in Britain until 1951.

WHO'S SCRYING NOW?

You've probably heard the expressions "dumb as a rock," "hard as rock," and "steady as a rock." But you had to come to Uncle John to hear "magical as a rock!"

ROCK OF AGES

In ancient Asia, agates were more than just pretty stones to collect. They were believed to be powerful magical tools. A yellow agate could lighten your mood. An orange or brown agate could put money in your pocket. A red agate could keep spiders away. And a black agate? Carrying one "guaranteed" victory in the sports arena. For thousands of years, agates have been also used for another magical purpose: *scrying*.

I SEE...A ROCKY FUTURE

Scrying is a form of fortune telling practiced by ancient cultures such as the Egyptians, Greeks, Celts, and Persians. Practitioners believe it's a way to see the past, the present, and even the future.

WHAT YOU NEED:
○ A polished agate

WHAT TO DO:
1. Find a quiet place.
2. Hold your agate up to a light.

3. Ask a specific question related to your past, present, or future.

4. Keep a steady gaze and a clear mind, and...wait.

5. In time—so the mystics say—truths will be revealed. And then the mystical forces inside the gemstone will magically project images into your mind.

6. Write down a description of the pictures that come into your mind.

7. Your gut feelings about the images will help you decide how the images answer your question.

Don't have an agate handy? Scrying can also be done using a mirror, water, or other clear polished stone or crystal. Gaze if you dare!

o　o　o

MAGICAL TUNES

If the title "Who's Scrying Now" sounded familiar, it's because Uncle John loves playing with songs, like these...

- *I'm So Lonesome I Could Scry*, by I. Nita Vision
- *An Even Whiter Shade of Pale*, by Sheesa Vampire
- *I Believe I Can Fly*, by Peggy Suss
- *We Gotta Get Out of This Place*, by N.A. Dungeon
- *I'm Feeling Hot, Hot, Hot*, by Bea Phoenix
- *I Only Have Eye for You*, by The Cyclops
- *Squirrels Just Wanna Have Fun*, by Thayer Knutz
- *I Put a Spell on You*, by I. Havawand

LITTLE-KNOWN LITTLE FOLK

. . . .

*Beware the dracs and portunes! But first, you'd
better find out what—and where—they are.*

SPECIES: Cluricauns
SPOTTED IN: Ireland
BEHAVIOR: These leprechaun cousins are rumored to
be tiny old men with terrible tempers. They come out at
night for a bit of fun, and, after a few drinks, have been
known to ride about on sheep and dogs. It's said that
they protect a family's wine cellar, but if the family makes
the cluricaun angry? The wine will taste like vinegar.

SPECIES: Dracs
SPOTTED IN: The river Seine, France
BEHAVIOR: These little elves shape-shift. They may
take the form of purple globs that float on top of the
water. Or they may form themselves into golden goblets
and rise from the river. If a human tries to grab one, he'll
be dragged underwater to the dracs' kingdom and forced
to work for seven long wet years.

SPECIES: Kobolds
SPOTTED IN: Germany
BEHAVIOR: Until the 1600s, many miners believed

kobolds were small goblins that lived underground and caused rock slides and cave-ins. Their favorite prank? Leading miners to ore that looked like copper or silver. When *smelted* (melted to purify it) the ore smelled awful, like garlic. Around 1735, a Swedish chemist named Georg Brandt realized the stinky ore was its own kind of metal. He named it *cobalt* after the legendary goblins. (Cobalt adds that lovely bright-blue color to teapots.)

SPECIES: Monaciellos
SPOTTED IN: Italy, near Naples
BEHAVIOR: Sturdy and broad like dwarfs, monaciellos dress like monks. (*Monaciello* means "little monk.") A little monk will only appear to a human who is in great need. They've been known to either turn bread into gold or to lead humans to treasure. But rumor has it that they have a warped sense of humor. They like to sneak around kitchens at night, raid refrigerators, and turn on faucets and stoves…and leave them on.

SPECIES: Portunes
SPOTTED IN: Great Britain
BEHAVIOR: Small and wrinkled, these fairies wear tattered coats, eat frogs roasted on sticks, and like to help out on farms. Sound useful? They are, unless a farmer insults one by offering to replace its grubby coat. Then the portune will drive the farmer's horses into the nearest swamp and laugh like a lunatic as the poor beasts try to get out.

THE MILKMAID'S HALLOWEEN

. . . .

An Uncle John's Totally Twisted Tale

THE MILKMAID LOOKED AROUND at the rundown farm where she lived. "I'm tired of these stupid chores," she said. "Milk the cows, feed the chickens, hoe the beans! Give me a break!"

She was ready to leave it all behind. But she was just a kid. How would she ever get enough money to flee the farm?

As she walked from the barn toward her house, she passed the pumpkin field. The fat orange pumpkins reminded her: Halloween was tomorrow! She could go trick-or-treating and collect as much candy as her milk pail would hold. Then she'd sell the candy to the other kids on the school bus.

"I'm a genius!" She grinned.

The next morning, she took the biggest milk pail she could find and headed up the road. As she crossed a bridge over the river, she could see the farm in the distance, spreading out over the valley. "I'll soon be leaving you for good!" she said.

She collected candy bars and lollipops at all of the houses on her road. Then she walked into town and knocked on every door. Soon all kinds of treats clanged

merrily in her milk pail. "When I sell this candy, I'll be rich," she said. "I'll buy a train ticket and head for Hollywood."

All evening she collected candy. As the pail filled up, she got even more excited. "This haul will bring in so much money, I can buy new clothes, too!"

Her dreams kept growing. She'd dye her hair bright orange and audition for *Milking with the Stars*. Once she got on TV, she'd be rich beyond her wildest dreams. All thanks to a pail full of Halloween candy.

The sky grew dark as she headed back out of town. Along the way, she spotted a caravan—not the gypsy kind, but the motor home kind that retired people toodle around in. The milkmaid knocked on the door, and a tall chicken-headed creature wearing a purple jogging suit answered.

"Yez?" asked the chicken head.

"Uhmm…nice costume?" said the milkmaid hopefully.

"Halloveen. Yez. Tank you," said the chicken head in a heavily accented female voice.

"Trick or treat?" The milkmaid held out her pail.

"Vwone moment," said the chicken-woman.

Behind the door the milkmaid heard something that sounded like feathers flapping, followed by a squawk. *Buh-kack!*

The door opened, and the chicken-woman in the jogging suit plunked an egg into the pail.

"That's not candy!" The milkmaid scowled.

"Candy iz bad for teeth." The chicken-woman opened her beak, showing a mouth full of tooth rot.

"Right. Thanks!" said the milkmaid, and she turned and fled.

By now, the milkmaid's arms were aching from carrying the heavy pail. But nothing could dampen her excitement. When she topped the last hill, she looked at the rundown farm that had been her home. "Soon, all of this will just be an unpleasant memory."

That night, the milkmaid counted the candy. "Five hundred eighty-five pieces of candy and one egg. By this time tomorrow, I'll be headed for Hollywood." She set the pail beside her bed and nodded off to sleep.

As the milkmaid slept, lollipops and butterscotch bites danced in her dreams. Weird techno-music that sounded like crinkling candy wrappers played over and over as the candy cha-cha-cha'd.

When the milkmaid woke up, she stretched. *Whew! Wacky dream*, she thought as she rolled over and peered into the pail. Then she gasped. The pail was filled with empty candy wrappers. A broken eggshell sat on top, and a trail of purple feathers led out her bedroom door.

"Gerta!" called her mother. "Get up, lazyshanks. It's time to milk the cow and feed the chickens!"

Moral: Don't count your candy before the chicken hatches.

THE END

THE ENCHANTED TOILET

ART BY JOHN GAFFEY

WORD WENT FORTH THROUGHOUT THE LAND THAT **UTHER PENDRAGON**, KING OF ALL ENGLAND, HAD DIED.

SO THAT NONE BUT THE TRUE HEIR MIGHT SIT UPON THE THRONE, THE WIZARD MERLIN WOVE A SPELL.

"BITTITY-BOPPITY..."

"... OOPS!"

"BETTER COVER THAT UP."

WHOSO SITTETH UPON THIS **ENCHANTED THRONE** AND TURNETH IT INTO A REAL THRONE IS RIGHTWISE, LEFTWISE, AND ALL OTHERWISE THE TRUE KING OF ENGLAND.

MANY TRIED... PRINCES, AND BARONS, AND KNIGHTS, AND SECOND-COUSINS-TWICE-REMOVED. BUT **THE ENCHANTED THRONE** REMAINED AS MERLIN HAD MADE IT—A TOILET.

ON THE DAY OF THE ANNUAL TOURNAMENT, SIR YECTOR ARRIVED AT THE CASTLE WITH HIS YOUNG SQUIRE, ZIT.

"ZIT! HELP ME INTO MY ARMOR."

"WAIT! I FEAR THAT I MUST GO."
"GO?"
"YES ... GO. NOW. FIND THE LOO!"

WITH SIR YECTOR OFF
TO THE JOUST AT LAST,
ZIT FOUND A QUIET
PLACE TO READ,

"ALL HAIL, ZIT, TRUE
KING OF ENGLAND!"
-THE END-

HOGWARTS: AN INSIDER'S GUIDE

*A BRI member visited the London studio where
the Harry Potter movies were made. She's no Rita Skeeter,
but she did uncover a few secrets!*

HOGWARTS SHOCKER

This may be a blow to aspiring witches and wizards, but
our insider says, "Hogwarts school doesn't actually exist."
A large miniature model of the castle was built for the
first few Potter films. The rest of the school consists of
sets at Warner Bros. Studios near London and parts of
historic English buildings.

Hogwarts' elegant corridors are really in historic
Gloucester Cathedral. The school's hospital wing and
library are actually parts of Oxford University's Bodleian
Library. The arch-ceilinged classrooms are part of Lacock
Abbey. And the school's Great Hall is the Great Hall of
Christ Church College (also part of Oxford).

THE GROWING GRYFFINDORS

There's a reason Harry, Ron, and the other Gryffindor
boys aren't seen stretched out on their beds in the final
films. The beds in their dorm are too short! They were
built when the actors were about 11 years old. Once the
actors hit their growth spurts, they were too tall to lie

down under the covers. So they had to be filmed sitting or reclining on their beds. Our insider had a quick sit-down on Harry's bed, and found it "too hard."

WHAT'S GREAT ABOUT THE GREAT HALL?

On the set, our insider saw many of the rich details you see in the movies: crystal goblets, silver cups and saucers, a podium topped with a fierce carved owl, and those fringed house banners dangling from the vaulted ceiling. In fact, the Hogwarts' Great Hall movie set was so closely modeled on the Great Hall of Christ Church that it looked like the real deal.

"But it's a wonder the hall passes fire codes," said our insider. Why? When the filmmakers asked Potter author J.K. Rowling if there could be electricity on the Hogwarts set, she said, "Certainly not!" So the hall is lit by firelight. Tall black candelabras line the tables. Huge metal bowls filled with fire hang from the ceiling and gargoyles spouting fire protrude from the hall's stonelike walls. "All that fire makes the place feel really magical!" said our insider. (We told you she was no Rita Skeeter.)

Our insider did notice something odd when dinner was served—"The food didn't magically appear on the tables," she said. "Waiters brought it."

Our insider was seated at the Slytherin table. That makes us wonder: Did someone *know* she was the type of person who would steal the table decoration? "It was a cheap wooden replica of the Slytherin coat of arms," she huffed. "I would never take the real thing! Honestly."

DUMB CLUCK

An Uncle John's Totally Twisted Tale

HENNIE HAD AN EASY LIFE. She was Mrs. Lean's only chicken, so she had the whole coop to herself. She rigged up a fan to keep herself cool, and she spread a soft blanket in her nest for sleeping. Mrs. Lean fed her a bowl of corn every morning. In return, all Hennie had to do was produce one egg a day. No chicken in the county had a more comfy setup.

Life is good, thought Hennie. *But maybe it could be even better!*

The next morning, Hennie stood in the chicken yard outside her coop. She watched as Mrs. Lean poured corn into a bowl.

"Is that all?" Hennie asked.

"That's the same amount I always give you," said Mrs. Lean.

Hennie cocked her head and eyed the bowl. "If you gave me twice as much," she cackled, "I could lay twice as many eggs."

Mrs. Lean thought for a moment. "I've been feeling a bit lean lately," she said. "Two eggs would be wonderful." So Mrs. Lean poured Hennie a double helping.

The next day Hennie still laid only one egg. "It takes a while to produce two eggs," she clucked. "Keep the feed coming, and soon you'll have your two eggs."

Mrs. Lean's stomach growled. She took the lone egg and went into the farmhouse to fry it sunny-side up.

Hennie ate a double serving of corn every day that week. By the end of the week, she was round as a Butterball Turkey, but she still laid only one egg a day.

Soon the overstuffed chicken was too pooped to walk into the yard and peck around. She lazed around in her nest day after day, until one day—nothing! Not a single egg.

Mrs. Lean peered into the coop. "Look at you!" she said. "You can hardly move. And I'm wasting down to skin and bones. I *must* have an egg today!"

"Tomorrow I will lay two," Hennie said. "I promise."

But there were no eggs the next day. Or the day after that. Mrs. Lean had to eat cracked corn instead.

"What about me?" asked Hennie.

"The more you eat, the fewer eggs you lay," said Mrs. Lean.

"I'll be laying double yolkers soon," said Hennie.

"Fat chickens are good for only one thing!" said Mrs. Lean as she closed the coop and locked the door. "I've always liked fried chicken better than eggs anyway."

A word from your storyteller: It's possible that Hennie immediately squawked out two fat eggs. It's also possible that Mrs. Lean wasn't carrying an axe when she returned to the coop. But…this *is* a cautionary tale about being greedy.

THE END

HOW TO
ATTRACT AN ELF

Elves are much smaller than humans and usually only show up in groups of two or three. The best way to attract them? Think small. Try luring elves to tea with this recipe, which makes three tiny cakes.

WHAT YOU NEED:

SUPPLIES
- Small bowl
- Whisk
- Spatula
- 6- or 12-cup muffin pan

INGREDIENTS
- ¼ cup unsalted butter
- ½ cup plus 1 tablespoon flour
- ¼ cup buttermilk
- 1 small egg
- ½ teaspoon vanilla
- ½ cup sugar
- ¼ teaspoon baking soda
- ¼ teaspoon salt
- ½ cup whipped cream (optional)

WHAT TO DO:

1. Preheat your oven to 350 degrees.

2. Use a bit of butter to grease three cups in the muffin pan. Then dust those cups with a little flour. Fill the muffin cups you're not using about halfway with water.

3. With an adult's help, melt the rest of the butter on the stovetop or in the microwave.

4. Whisk the buttermilk, egg, vanilla, and melted butter together. Add the flour, sugar, baking soda, and salt. Stir the batter until it's smooth.

5. Divide the batter equally in the three muffin cups. Then bake the elf cakes for about 22 minutes (or until they're set).

6. In the movie *Elf*, Buddy the Elf says, "We elves try to stick to the four main food groups: candy, candy canes, candy corn, and syrup." So, after the cakes cool, top them with whatever you have on hand that comes from one of the four elfin food groups.

Serve Elf Cakes with Magic Tea (page 101).

o o o

THE ELF OWL
An elf that hoots? Who knew!

- The elf owl is tiny—about the size of a sparrow.
- It nests inside natural cavities and woodpecker holes found in cacti in the southwestern United States and Mexico.
- If captured, the elf owl will play dead until it feels safe.
- In winter, the elf owl heads south. Why? The moths, crickets, and beetles it eats can't survive the cold.

BURN, BIRDIE, BURN

*You may have heard of the phoenix—the bird that lives forever
by catching fire and rising anew from its ashes.
Turns out that quite a few cultures share this myth.*

THE BENNU
PLACE: Egypt
LEGEND: The Egyptian Bennu was a golden bird that
looked like a heron. When the world began, it popped
up from the "primordial mud"—the gooey origins of all
life. The Bennu was favored by the sun god, Ra. It spent
a lot of time flying around gathering bits of myrrh—resin
from a thorny tree. Why? To build its own funeral pyre.
Every 500 years, the Bennu settled onto its pyre and
burned itself to ashes. Three days later, it rose from the
ashes to start the cycle again.

THE FENG HUANG
PLACE: China
LEGEND: The Feng Huang ruled over all other Chinese
birds. It had a colorful tail like a peacock and a sleek
head like a pheasant. In the beginning, there were two
Chinese firebirds, one male and one female. They stood
for the *yin* and *yang* of life—the balance in all things. In
time, the two birds merged to become one—a female.
She became the symbol of the Chinese empress. Unlike
other firebirds, the Feng Huang was born from fire only

once and lives forever, so she doesn't have to burst into flames again and again.

THE SIMURGH
PLACE: Persia
LEGEND: In Persia (now Iran), this fiery bird was said to be so old it had seen the entire universe rise and fall three times! The Simurgh was huge: big enough to carry off a whale. It had a dog's head, a peacock's body, and a lion's claws. In one legend, thousands of birds race for a single feather of a Simurgh. The 30 who complete the race find themselves trapped in its nesting place. They then realize they are part of the Simurgh—one with the world, at peace, and immortal. (Another version says they became one with the Simurgh because it *ate* them.)

THE ZHAR-PTITSA
PLACE: Russia
LEGEND: Glowing like a bonfire, Russia's Zhar-Ptitsa was a magical bird with red, orange, and yellow feathers. The Zhar-Ptitsa could light up the night sky, protect or heal with its magical feathers, and drop pearls from its beak as it sang. But this firebird was a bit of a thief. Night after night, it flew into the king's garden and snatched some of the golden apples of eternal youth that grew there. So a stable boy baited a trap with the bird's favorite treat: cheese soaked in beer. The bird chowed down and then wobbled drunkenly around the garden until the boy caught it.

MOVIE MAGIC

Your eyes aren't the only things being bamboozled at the movies. Sound-effects technicians called "foley artists" know all kinds of tricks to fool your ears, too!

RAIDERS OF THE LOST ARK (1981)
We Hear: A giant stone ball chasing Indiana Jones (Harrison Ford) out of a cave.
Actual Sound: A Honda Civic coasting on gravel.

JURASSIC PARK (1993)
We Hear: *T. rex* ripping apart an ostrich-like dinosaur called a *gallimimus*.
Actual Sound: A dog attacking a rope toy.

TITANIC (1997)
We Hear: Rose (Kate Winslet) clinging to a makeshift raft in ice-cold water while her hair freezes.
Actual Sound: The popping of ice crystals that have formed on frozen celery. "It worked out magically," said sound designer Christopher Boyes.

LORD OF THE RINGS: THE TWO TOWERS (2002)
We Hear: The huge Uruk-hai army yelling war chants and banging their chests before attacking Helm's Deep.
Actual Sound: 25,000 rowdy sports fans during a cricket match between New Zealand and England.

ICE AGE (2002)

We Hear: The mammoth walking through snow.
Actual Sound: A log dropping into a pit full of dirt and pebbles.

HARRY POTTER AND THE CHAMBER OF SECRETS (2002)

We Hear: A mandrake's deadly screams in Professor Sprout's class.
Actual Sound: A very hungry one-month-old baby crying, mixed with a woman's screams. The sound designer said the sound was "exotic enough so that you think, *Hmm, I've never heard anything quite like that before.*"

LEMONY SNICKET'S A SERIES OF UNFORTUNATE EVENTS (2004)

We Hear: Aunt Josephine's (Meryl Streep) house tumbling off a high cliff into Lake Lachrymose.
Actual Sound: This one is real. The filmmakers actually dropped a large dead tree on the house!

SPIDER-MAN 2 (2004)

We Hear: Doctor Octopus (Alfred Molina) moving his tentacles around or retracting them.
Actual Sound: The foley artists rolled and threw around motorcyle chains to make the sound of Doc Ock's arms moving. But when he retracts his tentacles (pulls them back into his body), that's the sound of heavy-gauge piano strings being pulled across metallic objects.

THE BOY WHO CRIED CELEBRITY

....

An Uncle John's Totally Twisted Tale

ONCE UPON A TIME...there was a boy who moved from Boring, Oregon, to Brooklyn, New York. After a week of being called the "Boring Boy from Boring, Oregon," he thought of a way to make himself seem more interesting: Celebrities. If he could show everyone photos of himself with stars (the celebrity kind, not the sparkly kind), they'd definitely be impressed.

At school the next day, the boy showed a photo to the kids at his lunch table. "Look who I had lunch with yesterday," he said. "Jackie Chan!"

The boy sitting next to him snorted. "You're standing in front of a poster for a Jackie Chan movie," he said. "See? It says 'Coming Soon' right behind your ear."

So the boy brought in another photo. "You're not going to believe this," he told the kids in history class. "Lady Gaga dropped by my house last night!" He showed them the picture.

"You're right," said the girl sitting behind him. "We don't believe it. Wanna know why? She wore that meat dress to the MTV Video Awards two years ago. If she was wearing a two-year-old meat dress, you wouldn't be sitting that close to her."

"Eew." Several kids pinched their noses shut.

The next day, the boy brought in a photo of himself with Tom Cruise.

"Okay, but for real," he said, pointing to the man in the grainy photo. "Tom Cruise!"

"Are you kidding?" said the class bully. "No way is that Tom Cruise! That guy isn't much taller than you."

"Tom's five foot seven," said the boy. "He just looks taller on those big movie screens."

That night, his friend Bill came over. The boy told Bill how everyone made fun of him when he showed his celebrity photos.

Bill nodded. "They think you're crying wolf," he said.

"Huh?" The boy scratched his head.

"You know. Like in the fairy tale. This kid wanted attention so he kept saying, 'Look! A wolf!' when there wasn't one."

"But—"

"And then, when a real wolf came to town, the kid yelled 'Help! Wolf!' but nobody believed him."

"What happened?" asked the boy.

"The wolf ate him."

"Bill, this is not helping," said the boy.

"Tell you what," said Bill. "I'll make a video of the two of us together and post it on YouTube."

"Really?" said the boy. "Thanks!"

The next day, everyone at school was talking about the video. "Great video of you and Bill Murray!" said one

kid, trying not to grin.

"Yeah. It's almost as believable as the one with Bill Murray washing dishes at that college student's party," said another kid.

"Or Bill Murray reading poetry to those beefy construction workers," said a third kid.

The girl from his history class shook her head. "Only the Boy from Boring wouldn't know that Bill Murray sightings are the biggest urban legend in Brooklyn," she said.

"Huh?" The boy's mouth gaped.

"Dude, Bill Murray stories are a dime a dozen. In every story, Murray shows up and does stuff with people, and then he says 'Don't tell anyone. They'll never believe you.' But Bill Murray doesn't *really* do any of those things. That's what makes them urban legends."

Just then, Bill Murray stopped by the school to see if the video had helped his friend. He was on his way home from rehearsing an off-Broadway production of *Peter and the Wolf*, and he was still wearing his wolf costume. When he saw all the kids making fun of his friend from Boring, he was so upset, he ate them. (But don't tell anyone. They'll never believe you!)

THE END

o o o

Twenty-five percent of Icelanders believe that elves "probably" or "definitely" exist.

BET ᴀɴᴅ ᴛʜᴇ BEAUTY

BY MICHELLE R. WEAVER

MY NAME IS BETTY BEASTE— "BET" FOR SHORT.

AND THIS IS MY FAMILY.

ONE DAY, PAPA CAME TO MY ROOM.

BOBBY, I HAVE GOOD NEWS!

I'M BETTY...

MAMA JUST HAD QUINTUPLETS...

UH HUH...

AND WE NEED YOUR ROOM FOR THEM.

WHA-!?

THE QUINTUPLETS

SO YOU'LL HAVE TO MOVE OUT.

WHERE AM I SUPPOSED TO GO?

Room For RENT

AND SO IT WAS I CAME TO LIVE WITH BELLO BELEZZA.

BELLO WAS VERY, VERY UGLY.

BUT HE HAD POTENTIAL.

I TAUGHT HIM TABLE MANNERS,

OMNOM NOMNOM

pfff

HOW TO STAY CLEAN,

AND HOW TO KEEP PESTS OUT OF THE CASTLE.

mrroooww!

FLUFFY!

OVER TIME, I DECIDED THAT LOOKS DON'T MATTER...

... IT'S WHAT'S INSIDE THAT COUNTS.

U.J.'S GUIDE
TO ENCHANTED PLACES

Writers dreamed up these places. But anyone can visit!

Emerald City: The capital of Oz may be the greenest city ever. A soldier with green whiskers guards the gate. Inside, people with greenish skin wear green clothes, hats, and shoes. What do they drink and eat? Green lemonade and green popcorn. (*The Wonderful World of Oz* by L. Frank Baum, 1900)

Cloudcuckooland: This Greek city was built in the clouds for birds, not people. Flocks of pelicans built the wall that surrounds the city. Saying someone is "living in Cloudcuckooland" means they're hatching foolish plans—like building castles in the air. (*The Birds* by Aristophanes, 414 B.C.)

Territory of Tuck: Look for this land in the Sea of Slops. It's right between the Mountain of Messes and Wastepaperland. The people who live here like to sell poisoned sweets to children. (*The Water-Babies* by Charles Kingsley, 1863)

Neverwhere: Have a taste for cat stew? It's the favorite dish in this candlelit world located below the streets of London. But brush up on rat language before you go. You'll need to speak it. Why? Because rats are rumored to be the most helpful creatures to be found here. (Neil Gaiman, *Neverwhere*, 1996)

Toyland: Nursery-rhyme characters such as Little Bo-Beep live in this country. So do toys with names like Big Ears and Miss Fluffy Cat. What lies beneath this happy land? Bogeyland, where crocodiles and hairy creatures with claws live. (*Noddy Goes to Toyland* by Enid Blyton, 1929)

Gort Na Cloca Mora: Cross a field strewn with boulders until you reach the edge of a forest. Knock three times on the biggest tree you find. When the leprechauns answer, follow them into their underground world. (James Stephens, *The Crock of Gold*, 1912)

Pumpkin Island: This island is home to the notorious Pumpkin Pirates. Huge pumpkins grow here. The pirates hollow them out and turn them into boats. Then they sail to sea to prey and pillage. (*True History* by Lucian of Samosta, circa A.D. 200)

The Midgewater Marshes: These swamps are infested with insects too tiny to see. But you can hear them! They make such a racket they're believed to be the evil cousins of crickets. (*The Fellowship of the Ring* by J.R.R. Tolkien, 1954)

Zuy: The elves of this kingdom have grown rich trading goods like leopard skins, music boxes, starch, and…suppositories. (*Kingdoms of Elfin* by Sylvia Townsend Warner, 1972)

THE BOY WHO LOVED DRAGONS

*What do you get when you cross dragons with
a kid who likes to doodle? Read on!*

BORED BY BOOKS

When Christopher's mom first tried to teach him to
read, he refused. He preferred doodling dragon pictures
and making up stories about them. He daydreamed
about dragons all the time: during trips in the car, in
the shower, even while he was pretending to do his
homework. Most people didn't think his obsession with
dragons would take him very far.

Christopher spent his teen years making up tales
about the dragons he loved. He started one story with
this question: "How might a young man find a dragon
egg?" Then he asked, "Where was the egg? How did it get
there?" Next he gave himself a "wild challenge": write a
whole book about a boy and his newly-hatched dragon.
He finished the first draft when he was 15 years old.

A ROAD SCHOLAR

Most writers have a tough time publishing their first
novel. Not Christopher. Why? Because his dad published
the book and had 10,000 copies printed. Then the family
hit the road. At the time, Christopher was 19. Instead of

going to college, he dressed up like a medieval storyteller and gave readings at bookstores. But pretty soon he was worried. His parents had quit their jobs and invested almost everything they had in his book. "As the saying goes, we really bet the farm," Christopher said. "It was down to the point where if we didn't sell enough books, we didn't have food on the table." His parents were even thinking about selling their house to raise money.

A DRAGON'S HOARD

What happened next may seem like a fairy tale, but it's true. A famous writer named Carl Hiassen bought Christopher's book in a store in Montana. Hiassen loved the book so much he gave it to his editor to read. The editor loved it, too. Before he knew it, Christopher had gone from worrying about money to accepting a six-figure advance from a publisher. (The exact amount isn't public knowledge, but six figures means at least $100,000.)

Christopher's first book made *The New York Times* bestseller list and sold more than 12 million copies. Its title? *Eragon.* That's right—the boy who loved dragons is Christopher Paolini. So far, he's written three sequels: *Eldest, Brisingr,* and *Inheritance.* In 2006, *Eragon* was made into a movie that grossed $249 million worldwide.

What does Christopher think about his success story? "If I wrote a book where all this happened to one character," he says, "no one would believe it." And that medieval costume he wore? "It will take some extraordinary event to ever get me back in that thing."

THE PIE PIPER

An Uncle John's Totally Twisted Tale

IT WAS THE GRAND OPENING of Boris the baker's Ye Old Pie Shoppe, and the whole village was there. The line of people eager to try Boris's pies stretched out the door and snaked all the way around the block.

"This line is too long," someone grumbled.

"These pies better be worth it," said another.

"We're bored!" whined the children.

Just then Peter Piper arrived. *All the pies will be gone before I get to the front of the line,* he thought. But then he looked down at his flute and had an idea. He edged his way into the shop.

"No cutting!" yelled a man.

"Boris the baker!" Peter waved his flute. "I will entertain your customers while they wait. Okay?"

"What's the catch?" Boris narrowed his beady eyes.

"No catch," said Peter. "Just a pie as payment." Peter pointed to a plump berry pie on the shelf. "I'll take that one there."

"Not so fast," answered Boris. "I'll pay. But first you must play."

"Fine," said Peter.

Before long, the people had forgotten the long line as they clapped and danced to Peter's tunes. When the last customer left the shop Peter went in to collect his pie. But every shelf was empty. "Where's my pie?" he demanded.

Boris came out from behind the counter and shoved Peter toward the door. "Sorry!" he said. "Sold out!"

"Hey!" Peter protested. "That's cheating, you cheating cheater."

"Oh, go pick a peck of pickled peppers," said Boris.

"What? What's a peck, for Pete's sake?" Peter asked.

"It's a unit of measure," Boris said, pushing Peter out to the sidewalk. "One quarter of a bushel!" And then he slammed the door in Peter's face.

Fuming, Peter stood there for a few seconds before he looked down at his flute. He ran a thumb over the switch at the bottom of the instrument. His eyes narrowed. The wizard who'd sold him the flute had told him it was magic. He'd warned him not to flip the switch to "on" except in times of great need. Peter's feet were sore from standing all day. His lips were swollen from piping and his stomach rumbled. He had a great need, all right. For pie! And he'd earned it. He'd give that cheating cheater Boris his just desserts.

Peter flipped the switch to "on" and the flute glowed with a golden light. "How about a peck of pies?" he yelled through the door. "How about a bushel AND a peck of pies?" He began to play his flute, and with every note a pie appeared. *Tweet!* A chocolate cream pie popped up in the flower pot. *Tweet!* An apple pie perched on the street lamp. *Tweet!* A lemon meringue pie popped into the gutter and gummed it up.

"Hooray!" shouted the villagers. "Free pie!"

Peter played while the villagers grabbed pies, stacked them high in their arms and in their wagons, and gobbled them as fast as they could. But for every pie someone claimed, two more pies popped up. Peter played faster. Mountains of pies shot toward the sky. Whipped cream waterfalls spilled from the rooftops and ran down the street. Meringue billowed and bubbled. Soon even the sunlight was blocked by sky-high stacks of pie.

"I can't eat anymore!" someone yelled.

"Ack, my belly!" moaned someone else.

"If I see ONE more pie, I'm going to hurl!"

"Stop!" Boris ran from his pie shop. "Stop playing!"

Peter stopped. "Why should I?" he asked. "You cheated me. Now you'll get your just desserts."

"It's not desserts," Boris grumbled. "It's deserts. 'Just deserts' means you'll get what you deserve. Not that you'll get dessert."

"Exactly!" said Peter. "This!" He waved his flute toward the pies and the pie-stuffed villagers. "Is what you deserve for cheating me out of my payment."

"This is YOUR fault?" The villagers glared at Boris. The baker backed away from the angry pie-sick crowd. "I'm sorry," he yelped. "I'll pay whatever you want, Piper. Name your price."

Peter grabbed a plump berry pie from a newspaper box. "My price," he said, "was a pie."

"I'll bake you a pie!" shouted Boris. "The best pie

ever seen in all the land."

"No need." Peter took a bite of the berry pie. Purple filling oozed down his chin. "This will do nicely."

"But my business," Boris whimpered. "It's done for. No one will want pie after all this."

"And who's going to clean up this mess?" someone yelled.

"Hmmm…" Peter looked at his flute. "I could bring in some rats to eat them."

But THAT'S another story.

THE END

∘ ∘ ∘

THE BLACKBIRD KNOWS
Heard about the 24 blackbirds baked into a pie for a king?
Here's what happened after they got out!

The King was in his counting-house,
Counting out his money.

The Queen was in the parlor,
Eating bread and honey.

The maid was in the garden,
Hanging out the clothes;

There came a little blackbird,
And nipped off her nose.

WEIRD WIZARDS

These real-life wizards take strange to a whole new level.

THE GEEZER. Artephius was a Spanish sorcerer who claimed to have a formula that would provide a very, very long life. First, he said, he visited hell to collect the fabled philosopher's stone. Then he used the stone to make the "elixir of life." Artephius shared his knowledge in a book called *The Secret of Prolonging Life* in which he claimed to be...1,025 years old!

THE HUMAN MAGNET. Robert Fludd was a "medical mystic" who lived in the 1600s. Fludd thought that the human body had magnetic poles, just like Earth does. One of his healing tools was a magnet made from human flesh. Fludd said that the best flesh for a human magnet came from "a body still warm, and from a man who has died a violent death." He believed a human magnet could cure disease. How? By attracting the disease to itself, the way an ordinary magnet attracts iron filings.

THE TALKING HEAD. Albertus Magnus, a Catholic bishop in the 1200s, is said to have created a "machine" shaped like a human head. He claimed that the head could answer any question he posed to it. The problem: He couldn't understand a word the head said, and it just wouldn't shut up. So Magnus destroyed it.

THE FRIEND OF DEMONS. The Catholic Church accused Peter of Abano (1250–1316) of learning the "seven black arts" from seven tiny demons. The clergy said Peter kept the demons inside a special jar and let them out whenever he performed magic. Historians say Peter of Abano was a scientist whose ideas were too advanced for the time. Among his crazy ideas? Celestial bodies—like the moon—affect nature. (You know, like making the tides rise and fall?) At the time, the Church thought angels or demons controlled such things. Peter was condemned to be burned at the stake. When he died in prison before the sentence could be carried out, the Church burned a stuffed dummy in his place.

THE SMOOTH CRIMINAL. Count Alessandro di Cagliostro convinced a lot of people that he could turn cheap metal into gold. Could he? Well, he wasn't known for being the most honest of men. For one thing, he wasn't really a count. His true name was Guiseppe Balsamo, and he grew up in the slums of Palermo, Italy. By age 14 he had robbed his uncle, and he was suspected of helping to rob and murder a wealthy priest.

Di Cagliostro was eventually charged with fraud, conspiracy, deception, and lying. He was sentenced to death, but Pope Pius VI spared his life. He died in prison around 1795. There's no proof that he ever turned metal into gold. But he did have some friends dress up like thugs and rob a gold merchant. The count's trickery earned him the nickname *Prince of Quacks*.

ALCHEMICAL FACTS AND FAKES

Which of these statements have been accepted at some time as factual, and which did we make up?

1. In A.D. 810, Jabir Ibn Haddyn wrote *The Complete Guide to Gibberish* to share his secrets with young alchemists.

2. Egypt's Emerald Tablet was said to reveal the secrets of the whole universe. In A.D. 32, a young boy found the tablet hidden in a cave. For the next five years he didn't talk and spent all his time studying the tablet.

3. Nicolas Flamel wrote a cookbook that included recipes for Stone Soup.

4. An alchemist named Saint Germain claimed he could calm bees and make snakes listen to music.

5. Three ancient arts became modern sciences— astrology became astronomy, natural magic became physics. And alchemy became chemistry.

6. Ancient Egyptians claimed that alchemy was not of this world. More than 3,000 years ago, visitors from outer space shared this secret science with mankind.

Answers on page 286.

COLOR ALCHEMY

Alchemists tried to turn lead into gold, but they weren't magicians. They were chemistry geeks who liked to mix things together to see what would happen.
Now it's your turn!

WHAT YOU NEED:

- Large red cabbage leaf
- Warm water
- Knife
- Large zipper-top plastic bag
- 2 clear plastic cups
- Vinegar
- Powdered laundry detergent

WHAT TO DO:

1. Chop the red cabbage leaf into tiny bits. (If you're likely to chop off your fingers, ask an adult to help.)

2. Put the chopped cabbage into a plastic bag with one cup of warm water and seal the bag.

3. Squeeze the bag until the water turns reddish blue, about three minutes.

4. Put ¼ cup of the blue water into each of the cups.

5. Add two tablespoons of vinegar to one cup. The blue water will change to pink.

6. Add one teaspoon of powdered laundry detergent to the second cup. The blue water will change to green.

WHAT'S GOING ON?

When mixed with an *acid* or a *base*, red cabbage water

changes color. It changes to pink when an acid (such as vinegar) is added and to green when a base (such as soap) is added. If you're an alchemist (or a chemist) you need to know how things will react when they're combined. Acids and bases are opposites, so when they're mixed together, they can *neutralize*, or cancel each other out.

Now that you know what color the water will be when an acid or a base is added, make more red cabbage water. Experiment to discover whether bubble bath, lemon juice, milk, and orange juice are acids or bases.

GROSS CHEMISTRY

o **Do you have acid breath?** Blow hard through a drinking straw into a cup of red cabbage water. Be sure to make lots of bubbles! If the water turns clear, it means you have acid breath. (Don't feel too bad. Breath has carbon dioxide in it, which is acidic.)

o **Ready to foam at the mouth?** Brush your teeth with baking soda toothpaste. Then take a sip of carbonated water (or soda). Open your mouth and let the foam roll! *Caution:* Do not swallow this stuff! Spit it out.

o **Green eggs, anyone?** Crack open an egg and separate the egg white and the yolk into two different bowls. Mix a little fresh red cabbage water with the egg white. (Egg white is a base, so it will turn green.) Fry or scramble your green egg. If you like yolks, plop the yolk on top after the green egg fries a little. Eat your fried green egg, or coax a family member into eating it.

WHO WAS THIS MERLIN GUY, ANYWAY?

Was the most famous wizard of all time a real person?
Good question, but we don't have a single answer…
we have three!

BLOODY BRITAIN

For several hundred years, Britain (present-day England, Scotland, Wales, and Northern Ireland) was part of the Roman Empire. Then, around A.D. 476, the Romans retreated. They left the British Isles in a bit of a mess, with lots of would-be kings and warlords fighting for control. The bloody, war-torn years after the Romans left have been called the Dark Ages.

Enter: Merlin. Legend says Merlin was a great wizard who could see the future. He told of a king who would unite Britain under one rightful ruler. Britain's real kings encouraged the myth. They wanted people to believe that their kings were destined to rule them. After all, Merlin had said so. But *which* Merlin?

MERLIN NUMBER 1: THE WARRIOR

People weren't sitting around writing down what happened during those bloody battles. But they did sit around the fire at night and tell stories. What is known

of early British history comes from stories passed from
one person to another for hundreds—even thousands—
of years. But written reports *have* been found about a
man called Merlin: Merlin Ambrosius.

This Merlin may have been a Roman noble named
Ambrosius Aurelius (or Aurelius Ambrosius) who stayed
behind in Britain when the Roman legions left. Aurelius
was a fierce warrior. He united the Britains and led them
to victory against Anglo-Saxon invaders. And then,
so the story goes, he gave up his power to a young man
named Arthur. Arthur became king and Aurelius was
his trusted advisor.

Could Ambrosius Aurelius have been the real
Merlin? The name Aurelius doesn't sound anything like
Merlin, but military leaders often took battle names
like *The Lion*, *The Hound*, and *The Leopard*. A merlin
is a type of falcon—a strong, swift hunting bird. So *The
Merlin* might have made a perfect nickname for a fighter.

MERLIN NUMBER 2: THE KID

There are also stories about a Merlin who was actually
called Merlin. When he was just a kid, this Merlin
was almost killed by a king named Vortigern. In the
mid-400s, Vortigern named himself High King of
Britain. Then he started building a fortress on a hill for
protection against Anglo-Saxon invaders. But the tower
kept falling down. Vortigern's wise men thought it would
help to kill a young boy and mix his blood into the
cement. (They did things like that in the Dark Ages.)

The wise men scoured the country looking for just the right boy. It wasn't easy. They thought the boy had to be "fatherless." Unfortunately for Merlin, the wise men arrived at his village just as he beat another kid in a ball game. The boy said something rude, like "Yo, Merlin! You may have a great throwing arm, but you don't have a dad!" It seems Merlin's mother had spread the story that his father was a "spirit" who sometimes visited her.

The wise men dragged Merlin off to Vortigern's fortress. Once he got there, he had a few things to say to the king. First he told Vortigern that there was a lake beneath the tower. Two dragons lived in the lake and their battles kept making the tower fall. Vortigern's men dug down to the lake and found the dragons fighting, just as Merlin had said. The king had his not-so-wise men put to death and gave Merlin their job.

Was this clever boy the *real* Merlin? Most of what is known about him came from a book called *History of the Kings of Britain* written by a monk named Geoffrey of Monmouth. Geoffrey claimed that the history was a translation of a "very ancient book written in the British language." Modern historians think Geoffrey's "history" was based on folklore and legend, not verifiable fact.

MERLIN NUMBER 3: THE NUTCASE

And then there's Lailoken—the Scottish Merlin. Legend says that Lailoken served a king named Gwenddoleu who had two huge birds that wore golden collars and ate four men a day. Lailoken was the king's bard. A court bard

had to be part poet, part historian, and part wise man.

Lailoken was living a rich life at court—he even had a gold collar of his own. In A.D. 573, King Gwenddoleu lost a bloody battle in southern Scotland. Three hundred of his soldiers were killed, and the enemy tossed their bodies into a mass grave.

Lailoken blamed himself for the defeat. He fled into the forest, where he lived for fifty years running around naked and talking to animals. The upside? The former bard gained the ability to see the future, including his own death. He predicted that he would die a "triple death." And he did. First, he was beaten with clubs by shepherds. Second, he fell over a cliff into a river. Third, he drowned.

Was this unlucky bard Merlin? Most of what is known about Lailoken comes from a few poems written hundreds of years after his death. There's also a fragment of a manuscript written by a Scottish holy man named Saint Mungo. The saint said Lailoken wasn't a wizard. He was a "hairy madman" who came to him once to confess his sins.

MERLIN BY ANY OTHER NAME...

Much of Britain's written history of the Dark Ages comes from Wales. In those writings, Merlin is called Myrddin. But some say Myrddin, or Merlin, isn't a name at all. It's a job title. A "merlin" was a top-class bard. So Merlin Ambrosius, a name that shows up on a Welsh list of bards, means "The Bard Ambrosius."

Others say the name Merlin isn't really the best translation of the Welsh word *Myrrdin*. The word was first translated into Latin as *Merdinus*. Geoffrey of Monmouth changed the "d" to "l" and came up with *Merlinus*. Why mess with Merlin's name? Geoffrey didn't want the greatest wizard of all time to have a name that sounds like the French word for "poop."

o   o   o

THE ONCE AND FUTURE WIZARD

Real or not, stories about Merlin have been around for more than 1,500 years. These are some of our favorites.

Knights of the Kitchen Table
by Jon Scieszka

The Young Merlin Trilogy
by Jane Yolen

Here Lies Arthur
by Philip Reeve

The Lost Years of Merlin
series by T.A. Barron

The New Magic Trilogy
by Pamela F. Service

The Book of Merlyn
by T.H. White

The Sword in the Stone
by T. H. White

Half Magic
by Edward Eager

Merlin Trilogy
by Mary Stewart

A Connecticut Yankee in
King Arthur's Court
by Mark Twain

ROTTEN ROBIN
AND HIS
SCARY WRENS

An Uncle John's Totally Twisted Tale

ROTTEN ROBIN AND HIS BAND of Scary Wrens lived in Scarewood Forest. They spent their days robbing the hooded crows, who taxed their patience, and giving to the whippoorwills, who threw the best parties.

One day, a scarlet tanager came to the forest. As he began to build himself a nest, he spotted a strand of pearls on the ground. "Jackpot!" said the scarlet bird. Flapping his black wings with all his might, he started lifting the strand up to his nest.

Rotten Robin spotted the small bird struggling with his treasure. "Wrens!" he said. "Those pearls would look better on Marian than on Mr. Scarlet."

The Scary Wrens took off. They flew to the stranger's nest and surrounded him in a tight circle. "Hey, Scarlet," said one of the wrens while slowly clicking the brass knuckles on his wing tips. "Robin wants doze pearls for his mate, Marian."

The scarlet tanager was annoyed. He didn't have size on his side, but he did have stubbornness and years of training in beak-kwon-do. "I think not," he said. "This bauble is mine. I found it fair and square."

"Sure," said another wren. "And we're about to take it—fair and square."

"Over my dead body," said the scarlet tanager.

The third wren chirped out a laugh. "If you say so," he said. Then he lunged at the tanager with his beak.

The scarlet bird did a front snap kick and sent the third wren flying. As the first wren lunged toward him, the tanager ducked to the side and swept his wing under the first wren's legs. The wren toppled off the branch and fell to the ground. Then the scarlet tanager did a somersault in the air, kicked out his legs, and sent the last two wrens flying.

Rotten Robin watched the fight from a higher branch. When the final wren fell, he flew down to face the scarlet tanager.

"Great!" said the tanager. "Another thief."

"You have some skill, Mr. Scarlet," said Robin. "You defeated my Scary Wrens without ruffling your feathers."

"Will," said the scarlet bird. "My name is Will."

Robin held out a wing. "I am Robin, leader of the Scary Wrens. How do you feel about hooded crows?"

"Ugh!" Will shook his neck feathers. "I left the Green Wood to get away from them."

"With a bird like you in our band, we'll soon rid Scarewood Forest of them," said Robin. "What say you?"

"And the pearls?" asked Will.

"You'll have to give a few to the whippoorwills," said Robin, "if you want to get into their parties. And, believe me, you want to. That's where I met my mate, Marian. She is the hottest robin in the forest."

And that's how Will, the scarlet tanager, joined Rotten Robin's band. Which caused a new problem— what to call the band. They couldn't be the Scary Wrens with a tanager in the mix, now could they?

THE END

∘ ∘ ∘

ROBIN HOOD: THE MAN, THE TIGHTS
What's worse? Making a living as a robber?
Or wearing tights in a forest?

- The Robin Hood legend may have been based on real-life British outlaws with equally fun names: *Fulk fitz Warin, Herewerd the Wake,* and *Eustace the Monk.*
- Some stories say that Robin Hood was named for the clothes he wore—a red cloak with a hood—which made him look a bit like a robin redbreast.
- Those green tights? Robin's legend has been around since at least the 1200s. Men did wear wool hosiery with their tunics then, but they weren't stretchy like the ones made today. In fact, they tended to sag.
- When actor Russell Crowe starred in *Robin Hood* (2010) he didn't wear tights. He wore leather pants. Why? "If you are going to be climbing trees, living in a forest, tramping through gorse bushes and brambles, how clever is it to wear a pair of tights?" Crowe said.

AND THE MAGIC NUMBER IS...

Fantasy series are a dime a dozen, but the numbers connected to these books are mind-boggling!

○ You'd have to be the worst kind of Muggle not to know about J.K. Rowling's Harry Potter series. But you might not realize that Rowling is the first author *ever* to become a billionaire by writing books. How rich is she? If Rowling were to spend $10,000 every day, it would take her more than 273 years to run out of money.

○ Think your teacher is long-winded? English professor J.R.R. Tolkien took 17 years to write his famous The Lord of the Rings series. When the book was finished, it was more than 1,200 pages long, and it weighed as much as a 10-pound dumbbell. Tolkien's publisher panicked—no one would buy a book that big! So the epic story was split into three parts and sold as a trilogy. The series has sold more than 150 million books, and the number grows every year.

○ Tolkien was good friends with another fantasy author, C.S. Lewis, who wrote The Chronicles of Narnia series. Although there are seven books in the series, all of them added together equal a measly 500 pages (less than half the number in Tolkien's masterwork). Still,

the Narnia books have collectively sold close to 120 million copies. That means every single child in the U.S. owns an average of 2 Narnia books.

o Madeleine L'Engle published more than 60 books in her lifetime, and 4 of those make up the Time series. But 26 publishers turned down the first book in the series, *A Wrinkle in Time*, before the 27th publisher accepted it. Why would so many editors dislike her book? Maybe because they're adults. "When I have something to say that I think will be too difficult for adults, I write it in a book for children," L'Engle said.

o Philip Pullman's most famous series is a trilogy called His Dark Materials. The series includes *The Golden Compass, The Subtle Knife,* and *The Amber Spyglass.* Pullman's numbers: He's written 30 books that have been translated into more than 40 languages. And he's won a half-dozen major awards and prizes. Why was Pullman drawn to writing fantasy? "I'm very lazy," he says. "If I need something, I just make it up."

o Garth Nix (author of the Seventh Tower and Keys to the Kingdom series) gets from 20 to 80 letters and e-mails every week. Does he answer them? "If I could answer each one in 5 minutes, to answer 80 e-mails would take me 400 minutes, more than 6 hours, which is basically a whole working day. That time would not be spent on writing, and I figure that the great majority of my readers would rather I worked on new books and stories rather than answering mail."

THE HAIRSTORY OF RAPUNZEL

by Will Strong

There once was a fair maiden named Rapunzel who lived in a tower.

There is very little to do in a tower.

Sigh.

Rapunzel had only two hobbies, brushing her hair and feeding the squirrels.

Have a nut Mr. Squirrel.

I love you.

Squeeeeak!

KLONK

So Rapunzel chopped off her hair, tied it to a bedpost, and climbed out the window.

Then she got stuck.

Help!

Somebody help me.

POOF!

Help is on the way. Just hang in here, kiddo.

That is so not funny.

POOF!

Nice!

IN A TRANCE

What do you get when you cross a wizard, a doctor, a guidance counselor, and a priest? A shaman!

TRIBAL WIZARDRY

Shamans have been around since the Stone Age, about 30,000 years ago. People were using stone tools then, but they hadn't invented gardening. When they got hungry, they hunted animals or gathered food such as nuts and berries and rutabagas. But when food was scarce, tribal shamans called on "spirit animals" to help make sure a hunt was successful.

Shamans also helped out when tribe members got sick. What could they do thousands of years before modern medicine? They called on "plant spirits."

Shamans may sound like ancient history, but they're not. Even now, in the age of grocery stores and doctors' offices, shamans are still on call all over the world.

OUT OF THIS WORLD

To find the knowledge needed to heal the sick or the wisdom to help people solve problems, shamans go into trances. A trance is an altered state of mind (sort of like being hypnotized, but without the watch).

While in a trance, the shaman goes on a "journey" to meet spirit guides. Those spirits are believed to have wisdom and knowledge that can aid people here in the ordinary world. How do shamans reach a trance state? There are a number of ways, but they're not for the untrained—so don't even *think* about trying them at home.

SHAKE, RATTLE, AND WOBBLE

In Siberia, shamans drum themselves into trances. They bang—for a very long time—on reindeer-skin drums. In India, shamans chant and rhythmically tap a stick on a buffalo's horn. (Horns still attached to live buffalo are not used, for obvious reasons.)

Other shamans shake rattles, lead group dances, or sway along to drumbeats while wearing animal costumes. After enough drumming, tapping, dancing, or swaying, the shaman enters an altered state of mind. (Imagine turning around and around until you fall down, but without the falling part.)

MAKE MINE WITH MUSHROOMS

Some shamans eat themselves into trances. When they need to heal someone or talk to dead ancestors, they gobble down special mushrooms that cause hallucinations, sweating, and twitching.

The mushrooms they use can be very expensive. Shamans who can't afford to buy them sometimes have to settle for "secondhand" mushrooms. What's a secondhand mushroom? First someone eats a "magic" mushroom. Next that person pees. Then the shaman

drinks the urine—it still contains enough "magic" to induce a trance.

SMOKE SIGNALS

When shamans of the Upper Amazon River area want to journey to the other world, they either eat tobacco leaves or smoke them. Imagine smoking five or six three-foot-long cigars in one sitting. That's what shamans do. They believe that while humans hunger for food, spirits crave tobbaco. So they use tobacco to lead them to the spirits. *Be warned!* Smoking can bring shamans to the door of death. There, they believe, they can meet with the spirits who will teach them.

WHAT'S GOING ON?

Experts say that "contacting spirits" doesn't fully describe what shamans do. So what are they up to? The Maori people of New Zealand call on the sacred spirit *mana*. The North America Iroquois call on the spirit *oki*, and the Sioux call on *wakan*. Many names have been used for the force a shaman encounters during a trance, but they all seem to refer to the same thing: the life force that connects all things. Could such a force exist?

In 1911, a German physicist named Max Planck discovered that there is an energetic "empty space" between atoms. This energy field is everywhere at all times. Today scientists call it the *Zero Point Field*. Hungarian scientist Ervin Laszlo believes the Zero Point Field carries information about everything that is or ever was or ever will be in our universe. To access that information, he claims, all you have to do is find the right frequency of energy. Shamans would probably say that is what they have been doing all along.

o o o

THE FORCE IS WITH YOU

Want proof? These two experiments seem to show the existence of a field or force connecting all things.

• A biologist wanted to know where memories are stored in the brain. So he trained some salamanders to do specific things. Then he took out their brains, ground them up like hamburger, and put them back inside their heads. Result? The salamanders went right back to doing what they'd been taught to do. That seemed to prove one thing: memory is not stored in the brain. So where is it stored? Perhaps outside the body, in the Zero Point Field, the *mana* or *wakan* of the shaman.

• In 2003, Shireen Strooker and 600 other people stood in a field. At the edge of the field, hundreds of drawings hung from a fence. Shireen pictured what she had drawn. *I am the creator of the drawing,* she thought. *I have to become one with the drawing, and it will pull me toward it.* Then she walked across the field straight to her drawing without bumping into a single person. What's so special about that? Shireen was blindfolded.

THE BATHROOM READERS' TAROT

Make your own set of fortune-telling cards,
with a special twist from Uncle John!

UNDERSTANDING THE TAROT

Mystics have been using tarot cards to understand life and foretell the future for centuries. No one's sure who made the first tarot deck. Rumor has it the tarot was created thousands of years ago by 17 magicians just after a flood wiped out all life on Earth. (Which begs the question: Why were *they* still alive?) But some say it might have been a French wig maker who published a book on the tarot in 1785. It's all kind of...mystical. And so is reading the cards. The "meaning" of each card depends on what the reader *thinks* the meaning means. See what we mean?

WHAT YOU NEED:
- Heavy paper (card stock or poster board)
- Scissors
- Markers
- Old magazines
- Glue stick

WHAT TO DO:
1. Cut out seven 5" x 7" cards from the heavy paper.
2. Label each card with one of the names from "Uncle

John's Totally Quacked Tarot Cards" (below).

3. Illustrate each card to fit its name and meaning using markers and/or magazine cutouts.

WHAT TO DO NEXT:

1. Once you've finished making your cards, it's time to read the future. First, decide what you want to ask the cards. Hold the question in your mind.

2. Shuffle the cards, and then draw three cards.

3. The cards you drew all relate to your question. The first card is about the past, the second is about the present, and the third is about the future. Like those ancient mystics did, listen to your gut as you decide how the cards answer your question.

4. *Warning:* If a card is upside down when you draw it, the meaning is reversed.

o   o   o

UNCLE JOHN'S TOTALLY QUACKED TAROT CARDS

THE PUPPY: *The Puppy* is always excited and ready for whatever comes his way. But if the card is upside down? When a puppy gets too excited, accidents happen!

THE JOHN: This card stands for wisdom, and wisdom comes when you take enough time to listen to what your gut tells you. As we all know, the toilet is the number one (and number two) place for peace and quiet. So

it's the perfect image for this card. If *The John* is upside down, be warned—you haven't been listening to your gut. And things are about to get nasty.

THE DUCKY: This card means you are one lucky duck. Something great is coming your way, and the "luck" will happen because of your prior actions. If *The Ducky* is standing on its head, you're out of luck for now. But keep trying! If you do, your luck will return.

THE CLOWN: It's time to do something surprising or even silly. If *The Clown* is upside down, watch where you step. You may end up with poo on your clown shoes.

THE PLUNGER: Nothing can resist *The Plunger!* This card is all about strength. If you draw this card, be strong, face your fears, and plunge away. If the plunger is upside down, remember that brute strength isn't always enough. Be nice. It helps.

THE DRAIN: This card means change. You're ready to move on to something different. But before you can, you may have to flush old habits down the drain. If *The Drain* is upside down? You'll be stuck in the muck for a while.

MR. BUBBLE-Y: This card stands for success and happiness. After all, who could be unhappy in a tub full of bubbles? But if *Mr. Bubble-y* is upside down, watch out! Your bubble is about to burst.

THE HARE'S SIDE OF THE STORY

An Uncle John's Totally Twisted Tale

TIMMY HARE WAS LOOKING THROUGH an old box in his grandfather's attic when he came across a newspaper clipping. "Slow and Steady Wins the Race," said the headline. "Patient Tortoise Beats Lazy Hare!"

Like everyone else, Timmy had heard the story of the race between the tortoise and the hare. But as he scanned the article, he got a shock: The lazy hare had been his *grandfather*.

"Grandpa!" Timmy yelled as he pelted downstairs. "You lost that race to the tortoise? I can't believe it!"

Grandpa folded his paws. "Never happened," he said. "No tortoise could ever beat me."

"But the newspaper—" Timmy began.

"Lies!" said Grandpa. "I won that race by a mile!"

"Then why—"

Grandpa frowned. "Sit down, Sonny Jim. I'll tell you the *true* story of the tortoise and the hare."

Timmy grabbed a carrot and sat on his grandfather's knee.

"I was the fastest hare of my day," Grandpa said. "And that's how I caught the eye of the cutest bunny in the forest.

"But that danged tortoise was always trying to

show off. He tried to make me look bad every chance he got. Then, one day, he challenged me to a race. I knew he'd try to cheat. How else could he beat a hare? But I accepted the challenge anyway."

Timmy took a big bite of carrot and snuggled down to listen.

"We drew a line across the road," Grandpa said, "right at the top of a hill. We planned to circle through the forest and across the bridge, and end up back at the starting line. But the tortoise said it wouldn't be fair to finish the race going uphill. So we drew the finish line at the bottom.

"The tortoise said, 'first one to the finish line wins!'

"Lots of animals gathered to watch the race," Grandpa said. "A porcupine counted down: 'On your mark, get set, go!'

"I darted from the starting line, going so fast I raised a dust devil. And I kept running the whole way—through the forest, across the field, over the bridge, and all the way back to the finish. All those things you heard about how I took a nap along the way or loafed around? Those are lies! I ran my heart out."

Grandpa was so excited his knobby knees bounced, and Timmy almost poked the old hare's eye out with the carrot. "Sorry, Grandpa!" He tucked the carrot into his pocket, just to be safe.

"I came around the final turn and everyone was cheering," Grandpa said. "Then I spotted that cheating tortoise. He was running *down* the hill, from the starting line straight to the finish! I ran faster and faster, but halfway down the hill, that tortoise tripped and rolled the rest of the way to the finish line. And, yes, he got there first, by a whisker. But he was shell up with those stumpy feet of his a-kicking the air."

"But that's not fair!" Timmy said.

"You said it, Sonny Bob," said Grandpa. "I protested long and loud. I ran a mile and that tortoise only ran fifty feet! But everyone loves an underdog. Makes a better story. At least now you know the truth."

"Thanks, Grandpa!" Timmy hopped down from Grandpa's lap and headed to the kitchen.

Grandma Hare was putting the top crust on a cabbage pie. She smiled at Timmy. "Your grandpa is a great storyteller," she said.

"He sure is," Timmy said. "I'm glad to learn the truth about that race."

Grandma laughed and patted Timmy's head. "The truth?" she said. "Well, I can swear that at least one part of Grandpa's version is true."

"Which part?" asked Timothy.

"He caught the eye of the cutest bunny in the forest that day." Grandma winked. "And I married him, even though he does talk faster than he runs!"

THE END

WITCH HUNTS

In Medieval times, you could be accused of witchcraft at the drop of a hat—even if the hat wasn't black and pointed.

THE WITCH: Walpurga Hausmannin, Germany, 1587
SUSPECTED BECAUSE: She was elderly, and she had gnarled fingers and garlic breath.
ACCUSED OF: The death of at least 40 babies, 2 women, 8 cows, 1 horse, a passel of pigs, and a gaggle of geese
VERDICT: Guilty. For her crimes, Walpurga was stabbed five times with a red-hot poker, and her right hand was cut off. She was burned at the stake, and—so she couldn't come back from the dead—her ashes were dumped in a raging river.

THE WITCH: Marguerite Carlier, France, 1612
SUSPECTED BECAUSE: She was proud and outspoken.
ACCUSED OF: Killing animals and causing men misery
VERDICT: Guilty. Marguerite was banished and sent away from her family. She spent seven years in exile.

THE WITCH: Anna Pedersdotter Absalon, Norway, 1590
SUSPECTED BECAUSE: Her husband removed holy images from Catholic churches. (He was a bishop and a man, so she must have made him do it.)
ACCUSED OF: Killing a young boy with a bewitched biscuit, turning a servant into a horse and riding her to

a witch's sabbat, and plotting a storm to wreck a bunch of ships and flood the town
VERDICT: Guilty. Anna was burned to death.

THE WITCH: Alice Kyteler, Ireland, 1324
SUSPECTED BECAUSE: She was rich and a lot of people didn't like her.
ACCUSED OF: The death of four husbands and owning "terrible items," including body parts of an infant, the fingernails and toenails of corpses, skulls of robbers, and candles made of human fat
VERDICT: Guilty. Alice escaped before her execution.

THE WITCH: Anna Pappenheimer, Bavaria, 1600
SUSPECTED BECAUSE: She was the daughter of a gravedigger and the wife of a toilet cleaner.
ACCUSED OF: Witchcraft, murdering children to make an ointment from their bodies, and flying
VERDICT: Guilty. Her flesh was torn with hot tongs, and then she was impaled, tied to the stake, and burned to death.

THE WITCH: Nisette de Pas-de-Calais, France, 1573
SUSPECTED BECAUSE: Perhaps because she'd been married four times
ACCUSED OF: Witchcraft
VERDICT: Guilty. Flogged and banished after receiving the *chapeau d'etoupe*—a circle of flax or hemp was put on her head and then set on fire.

THE WITCH: Neele Ellers, Netherlands, 1550
SUSPECTED BECAUSE: She had scars said to be the "devil's mark." Her mother and grandmother had been accused of flying 100 miles a night (without a plane). Oh, and she owned land a neighboring man wanted.
ACCUSED OF: Bewitching a young girl to faint and puke horse hair, cursing butter so it would not churn, and knocking men into ditches
VERDICT: Innocent. Neele was released, but 40 years later she was accused again and executed.

THE WITCH: Alison Device, England, 1612
SUSPECTED BECAUSE: Her grandmother was 80 years old, blind, "ugly," spiteful, and outspoken, so...Alison was probably a witch, too.
ACCUSED OF: Giving her soul to the devil in return for having whatever she wanted, owning a hellhound, giving blood from under her left arm to a dog spirit named Tib, causing the death of an enemy's daughter, and extracting teeth from skulls
VERDICT: Guilty. Alison was hanged, and her grandmother, Elizabeth, was imprisoned in the dungeon beneath Lancaster Castle, where she died.

THREE FACTS ABOUT WITCH TRIALS

1. Most of the accused were female and poor.
2. An accusation was enough to convict a witch. No proof of guilt was needed.
3. Denial of guilt was seen as...further proof of guilt.

DO YOU BELIEVE?

A few quotes on magic and the land of fairy.

"Some things have to be believed to be seen."
— **Ralph Hodgson, poet**

"Imagination is the true magic carpet."
— **Norman Vincent Peale, minister**

"Many secrets of art and nature are thought by the unlearned to be magical."
— **Francis Bacon, scientist/ statesman**

"Everything is miraculous. It is a miracle one does not melt in one's bath."
— **Pablo Picasso, artist**

"Fairyland is nothing but the sunny country of common sense."
— **G.K. Chesterton, author**

"Disbelief in magic can force a poor soul into believing in government and business."
— **Tom Robbins, author**

"The universe is full of magical things, patiently waiting for our wits to grow sharper."
— **Eden Phillpotts, author**

"There may be fairies at the bottom of the garden. There is no evidence for it, but you can't prove that there aren't any."
— **Richard Dawkins, biologist**

"I think that people who can't believe in faeries aren't worth knowing."
— **Tori Amos, singer**

GRIM TALES FROM THE BROTHERS GRIMM

Jacob and Wilhelm Grimm may be famous for writing fairy tales, but they would never be hired to write Disney movies. Here are a few of our favorite "Grimm" storylines.

THE GIRL WITHOUT HANDS

The miller has fallen on hard times. He needs money fast. So, what does he do? He makes a deal with the devil. In exchange for wealth, the devil can have whatever he finds standing behind the mill. The problem? The miller's daughter is standing behind the mill when the deal is struck. When the daughter refuses to go along with the trade, the devil makes her dad chop her hands off. He does, and she's had enough. She packs her severed hands on her back and sets off to make her own way in the world. After all, she couldn't do much worse than dear old Dad.

RAPUNZEL

The fair Rapunzel has been trapped in a tower by a wicked sorceress. One day, a prince climbs up her long, long hair into the tower and asks her to marry him. She thinks that's a great idea, until...the sorceress finds out, cuts off her hair, and casts her out of the tower. When the young prince returns, the sorceress tricks him into climbing up the severed tresses. Then she tells him that his beloved is gone. "The cat got her," cackles the sorceress, "and will scratch your eyes out as well." Grief-stricken, the prince throws himself from the tower, right into a bed of thorns. The thorns pierce his eyes and blind him. After that, the prince wanders into the forest where he can find nothing to eat but grass and roots.

THE UNGRATEFUL SON

A man and his wife are about to eat a roasted chicken when the man sees his dad coming down the lane. Being the selfish sort, the man hides the chicken. Bad idea. When he takes it out again, it has turned into a giant toad. The toad jumps on his face and stays there...for the rest of his life. He has to feed the toad every day to keep it from eating his face off.

THE WILLFUL CHILD

Once there was a boy who would never do what his mom wanted him to do. Apparently, God didn't like his attitude, because he made the boy so sick no doctor could cure him. The boy died. He was buried, but his arm kept popping up out of the grave. No matter how many times the grave tenders tossed dirt on that arm, *pop!* There it was again. So the boy's mom went to the grave and beat the arm with a stick. After that, the boy settled down to his eternal rest. (We told you these stories were grim.)

HANSEL AND GRETEL

There's a famine in the land. The woodcutter worries that he won't be able to feed his wife and two children. What does his wife say? "Early tomorrow morning we will take the two children out into the thickest part of the woods, make a fire for them, and give each of them a little piece of bread. Then leave them by themselves and go off to our work. They will not find their way back home, and we will be rid of them." (Thanks, Mom.)

RED RIDING HOOD

A sweet little girl goes to visit her sick grandmother. Sadly, a wolf has eaten Grandma, and when Red Riding Hood shows up, he gulps her down, too. The end? No. A woodsman hears loud snores coming from Grandma's house (apparently the wolf snored when his belly was full). Finding the wolf in Grandma's bed, the woodsman hacks him open with scissors, and then pulls out Red Riding Hood and Grandma. The sweet little girl gathers up a bunch of heavy stones. She stuffs them into the wolf's belly and, when he tries to run, he falls down dead.

THE END?

Not all fairy tales end with "and they lived happily ever after." Some of the Grimm brothers' stories ended with this lively little rhyme:

My tale is done, a mouse has run.
And whoever catches it can make for himself from it
a large, large fur cap.

THE PRINCESS AND THE PEASHOOTER

An Uncle John's Totally Twisted Tale

ONCE THERE WAS A PRINCE who wanted to find a princess worthy to marry him. To be good enough for his royal self, she had to be a one hundred percent pure-blooded princess with a capital P. So the prince hit the road. He traveled to every kingdom marked on the royal map, even one that turned out to be a post office box. The weary prince checked out princess after princess. But no matter how pretty or polished, there was always something *not quite right* about every princess.

The prince came home with his bum dragging. He flopped down on his goose-down mattress, fell into a deep sleep, and slobbered on his pillow. As the prince slept, a storm swept down from the mountain. Thunder smashed. Lightning sizzled. In the middle of it all, something that sounded like hail started pinging against his window.

"Oy!" A voice called. "Up in the tower! Open up. It's frumping wet out here!"

The prince rolled over and blinked. *Ping! Ping!* With his spit-soaked pillow stuck to his cheek, he stood up, stumbled to the window, and threw open the sash.

"Who dares disturb my royal slumber?" he called.

Ping! Something whizzed past his ear. The prince squinted into the stormy night. At the bottom of the tower stood a princess wiping wet bangs out of her eyes.

"Are you serious?" she yelled. "Open up, or the next one's going right between your highness's squinty eyes!"

As the prince watched, she lifted something that looked like a peashooter to her lips.

"Hang on!" He slammed down the sash, thumped down the stairs, and yanked open the front door.

The princess strode into the cavernous hallway shaking off water like a mongrel dog.

"Hey!" the prince yelped. "This nightgown is silk!"

"Sorry." The princess tucked the peashooter into a pocket hidden in the folds of her soggy gown. "So, do you think I could have a place to sleep for the night?"

Just then, the queen swept into the hallway. "What is the meaning of this intrusion?" she demanded.

The prince waved a hand at the dripping girl. A puddle had formed at her feet.

"This princess shot peas at my window!" he said. "And then she threatened to shoot *me!*"

"Really?" The queen's eyes went wide. Then she put an arm around the girl's shoulders and ushered her toward the fire still smoldering in the front room.

"Sit down, dear." The queen pulled up two chairs.

The prince warmed his hands at the fire, watching the princess warily from the corner of his eye. For all he knew, she might take out that peashooter again. She wasn't like the other princesses he'd seen. In fact, there was something about her that reminded him of his mother. What was it?

"So," the princess settled into the chair. "I was hoping you might have a spare bed for the night."

The queen clapped her hands in delight. "Do you know, before the king and I wed, his horrible mother forced me to sleep on top of twenty mattresses. I nearly had a nosebleed!"

"You're kidding! Why?" asked the princess.

"She had put a pea beneath them." The queen snorted. "She believed that only a *real* princess would have skin delicate enough to feel a pea through twenty mattresses."

The queen leaned closer and whispered. "Don't tell the king, but I tricked the old bat. I peeked through the keyhole and saw her hiding the pea. I slept like a log that night. But in the morning I told her I hadn't slept a wink because something kept poking me in the back."

"Mother!" the prince huffed. "Are you not of royal birth?"

The queen glared at her son. "Of course I am. But what is this? The Dark Ages?"

"Yes, Mother." The prince nodded. "Yes, it is."

"Oh. Well…" She waved a hand. "Anyway, after our wedding, the pea was put into the Royal Museum. Once you marry the prince, I'll have to keep an eye on you." She winked at the princess. "I wouldn't want the royal pea to end up in your peashooter."

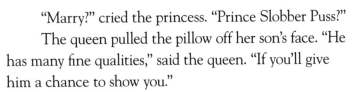

"Marry?" cried the princess. "Prince Slobber Puss?"

The queen pulled the pillow off her son's face. "He has many fine qualities," said the queen. "If you'll give him a chance to show you."

The princess fingered the peashooter in her pocket, and the prince scooted behind his mother's chair.

"Well, he did let me in out of the rain," said the princess. "So even though he's a bit of a prat, he must be a good judge of character. Otherwise, he'd have turned me away, what with the peas and the mud and the threats." She grinned.

That's when the prince saw it: *perspicacity*—that's what this princess had. Just like his mother. The queen could see beyond outer appearances to the truth. Time after time his mother had saved his father from blunders that would have ruined the kingdom. *Perspicacity* was what the other princesses lacked, even though they were much less grubby and prone to violence. At last, the prince knew just what he wanted: a girl just like the girl who had married dear old Dad.

It took him a while to convince her. First, he had to learn to use a peashooter as well as the princess did. Then he had to stop drooling on his pillow when he slept. But in time, they had a fairy-tale wedding.

So our tale ends, with the pea still on its royal blue pillow in the Royal Museum. Unless, of course, you-know-who has stolen it.

THE END

HAVE BROOM, WILL TRAVEL

Which enchanted ride would you chose?

MAGIC CARPET
PROS: Room for a crowd, very fast, beautiful
CONS: No protection from the weather, expensive, no seat belts
THE LORE: The biblical king, Solomon, was said to have had a magic carpet that measured 60 miles on each side. It was made of green silk and woven through with pure gold threads. Who and what went along for the ride? Iron stoves, huge stone pots, horses and other animals, the king's personal attendants, and…his entire army.

BROOM
PROS: Affordable, versatile (*Sweeps and Flies!*), fits perfectly in any broom closet
CONS: Uncomfortable to ride, no protection from the weather, splinters
THE LORE: In Germany, witches were said to have ridden on forks, shovels, and demons before they started flying on broomsticks. Why brooms? They could "sweep their tracks from the sky." But some witches rode their brooms with the sweeping end first. Then they'd stick a candle in the broomstraw to light their way.

(Headlights!) Ringing church bells are supposed to be able to knock a rider right off a broom, so this may not be the safest mythical mode of travel on Sundays.

WIZARD'S STAFF

PROS: Doubles as a weapon, has decorative options like crystals, performs other magical feats

CONS: Too long to conceal, but as easy to accidentally leave behind as an umbrella

THE LORE: Some say a wizard is much weaker without his staff. Others argue that the staff taps into the power inside the wizard. It stores that power, kind of like a magical battery. So when a wizard needs his staff, it's... eveready.

PEGASUS

PROS: Great conversation starter, good companion, operates on land or in air

CONS: Has to be fed and brushed, and its poop has to be cleaned up

THE LORE: The legendary winged horse boarded for a while in the stables of the Greek god Zeus. But after a while, Zeus stuck the creature in the night sky as a starry constellation. Unfortunately, it's upside down.

GRYPHON

PROS: No one's going to chase you if you're flying on a beast with a lion's body and an eagle's head and talons.

CONS: If you're wearing gold, it will rip you to shreds

and take your gold to line its nest.

THE LORE: Gryphon stories have been around more than 2,000 years. The creatures are rumored to have lived in Asia, mostly near the Gobi Desert. Gryphons have a lion's body and the head, wings, and claws of a giant eagle. Gryphons divided their time between snacking on horses and keeping a tribe of one-eyed miners called the Arimaspi from stealing their gold.

DRAGONS

PROS: Those leathery bat-like wings are fast. Can sometimes be persuaded to toast marshmallows.
CONS: Prone to snacking on roasted knights and kidnapping fair maidens.
THE LORE: Chinese dragons: wise and lucky. European dragons: cruel and greedy. Fossils have been found of animals with a long tail, huge teeth, and claws at the ends of their wings. Dragons? Nope. Just pterosaurs, but a huge flying reptile is pretty magical, too.

FAIRY WINGS

PROS: Lightweight, pretty
CONS: Attached to fairies, prone to shedding fairy dust (which may cause allergic reactions). *Achoo!*
THE LORE: It's said that fairy wings are made of shifting light, emotion, and energy. Plus, they're just for looks. Fairies don't actually use their wings to fly. They wish themselves wherever they want to go. So unless you can do that, don't bother stealing a pair of wings.

HOW TO BAMBOOZLE A TROLL

Trolls might look scary, but we hear it's easy to get the best of them. Just try one of these tricks!

1. Trolls sometimes try to pass for human, but they sleep during the day to avoid sunlight. When you come across a suspected troll napping, throw open the blinds. Some trolls will immediately turn to stone. Others will pull the bedcovers over their heads. If either of those things happen, you'll know you're dealing with a troll.

2. Trolls love to build things. The next time one bugs you, give it the biggest LEGOS set you can find. That will give you plenty of time to escape.

3. Many trolls have two or three heads. There's even a story about a troll with 121 heads! If you need help with math homework, find a multi-headed troll. Give each head a different problem to solve. The troll will be too busy to bother you, and your homework will be done before you know it. (*Warning:* Never give two heads the same problem to solve. They'll get different answers and argue about which one is right.)

4. All trolls are compulsive and like to sort things into piles and stacks. Next time your room's a mess, invite a troll to visit. It won't be able to resist tidying up.

5. Think *dogs* like sticks? Trolls love them. You may think they want to hit you over the head with those clubs they carry. They don't. They want you to throw the clubs so they can chase them. (You know, like a dog would.)

6. Trolls always have long matted hair that covers everything but their noses. If you need to escape from a troll, give it a hairbrush and a mirror. Then run!

7. Like elves, trolls can be friendly or cruel. It all depends on how you treat them. If you want the trolls in your life to be nice, you have to be nice to them first. They will follow your lead.

8. Let's face it, trolls smell horrible. Cologne would help, but trolls *like* to smell bad, so they won't wear it. There's a simple solution: Give the troll a bottle of toilet water (*eau de toilette* if it's a French troll). Toilet water is actually watered-down cologne, but trolls don't know that. The troll will think it's water from the toilet, and it will sprinkle the stuff all over itself.

9. Want a surefire way to enjoy a troll-free life? Trolls hate being around people. So surround yourself with lots of (non-troll) friends.

TIKKI TIKKI WHO?

....

An Uncle John's Totally Twisted Tale

A YOUNG HUSBAND AND WIFE were trying to decide on a name for their second son. "Have you ever heard the story of Tikki Tikki Tembo?" the woman asked. "It's about two brothers in China. One was named Sam, just like our son. The other's name was Tikki Tikki Tembo No Sarimbo Hari Kari Bushkie Perry Pem Do Hai Kai Pom Pom Nikki No Meeno Dom Barako."

"That's quite a name," the man said. "But kind of hard to remember."

They thought for a long time, but couldn't decide on a name. "I love Sam, but his name is so plain," the woman said. "I want this one to be special. Let's look in a celebrity magazine."

The magazine had lots of photos of men with names like Luke and Troy and Brad and Zach and Miles. And three more guys named Brad.

"Ho-hum," the woman said. She yawned, then picked up another magazine: *TV Guide.*

"Oooooh," she said. "There are some great names in here. Unusual ones, but memorable!"

She started listing the names of her favorite shows: *The Vampire Diaries, American Idol, Dancing with the Stars...* "I just can't decide," she said.

A few years later, Sam and his little brother were

playing soccer in the yard. Sam kicked the ball so hard
that it sailed over the fence. His little brother ran after it.
As he crossed a large field, he fell into a hole. It was an
old well, and so deep that Sam couldn't reach him.

"Help!" cried the boy. "It's really cold down here!"

"Don't worry!" Sam yelled. "I'll get Dad."

Sam sped home and ran into the house. "Dad!
Come quick! Vampire-Diaries-X-Factor-Biggest-Loser-
American-Idol-Wheel-of-Fortune-Survivor-Dancing-with-
the-Stars has fallen into a well!"

Dad leaped out of his chair. "Did you say that
Vampire-Diaries-X-Factor-Biggest-Loser-American-Idol-
Wheel-of-Fortune-Survivor-Dancing-with-the-Stars fell
down a well?"

Sam gulped for air. "Yes," he said.

"Let's go!" Dad said. He called to his wife. "Honey,
Vampire-Diaries-X-Factor-Biggest-Loser-American-Idol-
Wheel-of-Fortune-Survivor-Dancing-with-the-Stars has
fallen into a well. Hurry!"

They ran to the well. Dad looked down into the
darkness. "Are you all right, Vampire-Diaries-X-Factor-
Biggest-Loser-American-Idol-Wheel-of-Fortune-Survivor-
Dancing-with-the-Stars?"

"I'm very cold and wet," came a small voice. "Please
hurry and get me out. I've been down here a long time."

Dad could not climb down the well. The walls
were too steep and slippery. "We need a ladder," he said.
"Hang in there, Vampire-Diaries-X-Factor-Biggest-Loser-
American-Idol-Wheel-of-Fortune-Survivor-Dancing-with-

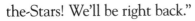

the-Stars! We'll be right back."

"Hurry!" called the boy. "I'm freezing!"

Dad ran to the neighbor's house. "My son has fallen into a well," he cried. "Do you have a ladder?"

"Which son?" asked the neighbor. "Sam?"

"No," said Dad. "The little one—Vampire-Diaries-X-Factor-Biggest-Loser-American-Idol-Wheel-of-Fortune-Survivor-Dancing-with-the-Stars."

"Oh, no!" said the neighbor. "I'll get my ladder."

"Hurry!" said Dad. "Vampire-Diaries-X-Factor-Biggest-Loser-American-Idol-Wheel-of-Fortune-Survivor-Dancing-with-the-Stars has been down there for some time. He's very cold and in danger of freezing."

The neighbor's wife came into the garage. "What's all the trouble?" she asked.

"Vampire-Diaries-X-Factor-Biggest-Loser-American-Idol-Wheel-of-Fortune-Survivor-Dancing-with-the-Stars has fallen into a well," the neighbor told his wife. "We have to hurry to save him."

"Poor little Vampire-Diaries-X-Factor-Biggest-Loser-American-Idol-Wheel-of-Fortune-Survivor-Dancing-with-the-Stars," said the neighbor's wife. "I'll help."

They all hurried back to the well. The neighbor scurried down the ladder and carried Vampire-Diaries-X-Factor-Biggest-Loser-American-Idol-Wheel-of-Fortune-Survivor-Dancing-with-the-Stars up. The boy was shaking, and his skin was icy cold. His pulse was slow, and he couldn't speak. They rushed him to the hospital.

"If he'd been down in that well much longer, he

would have died," said the doctor. "What took so long?"

"His name." Dad shook his head. "It took ten times as long to explain what had happened."

"Maybe it's time for a nickname," said the doctor.

Two years later, Sam and Biggest Loser's mom gave birth to twin boys. They named them Brad and...Brad.

THE END

∘ ∘ ∘

WHAT'S IN A NAME?

There are at least 500 fairy tales that include a mysterious helper who demands a terrible price—unless the hero guesses his name. Here are our top ten magical helpers.

1. Rumpelstiltskin (Germany)
2. Tom Tit Tot (England)
3. Hoppentînken (Germany)
4. Whuppity Stoorie (Scotland)
5. Silly go Dwt (Wales)
6. El Enano Saltarín (Spain)—in English the name means *The Jumping Midget*
7. Peerie Fool (Orkney Islands, Scotland)
8. Ferradiddledumday (Blue Ridge Mountains, U.S.A.)
9. Minnie Merran (Shetland Islands, Scotland)
10. Irnst Jacobs, the Werewolf of Vietlübbe (Germany)

MOTHER GOOSED

Uncle John thinks it's only fair to make fun of fairy tales.

Q: Why was Bo Peep surprised when it took three sheep to make one sweater?
A: She didn't know they could knit.

Q: Where did the three blind mice go after the farmer's wife cut off their tails?
A: To the retail store

Q: Which fairy tale animals are the rudest?
A: The three Billy Goats Gruff. They're always butting in.

Q: What did Baby Bear call his grandpa after Goldilocks stole his false teeth?
A: Gummy Bear

Q: Which fairy tale star wears a coat all winter and pants all summer?
A: The Big Bad Wolf

Q: Why did the little pig go to the restroom?
A: So he wouldn't wee wee all the way home.

Q: Why did the Frog Prince need life insurance?
A: Because he croaked every night.

Q: What grew down when it grew up?
A: The Ugly Duckling

Q: Why does everyone keep secrets from the Three Little Pigs?
A: Because they're squealers.

SIR, WAIT, LET'S NOT JUMP TO CONCLU—

THE SKY *IS* FALLIN'!

EVERYONE!

LISTEN UP! THE SKY IS FALLIN'! GET OUT WHILE YOU STILL CAN!

AND SO I RAN

SIR?

TO EVERY FLOOR IN THE BUILDING

WARNING MY EMPLOYEES,

SIR...

WAIT!

SIR!

SIR!!

OFFICER FOXY

WHO IS RESPONSIBLE FOR THIS DISTURBANCE?

LOOK HERE, OFFICER. THE SKY IS FALLIN', AND I HAD TO WARN EVERYONE TO EVACUATE—

HE IS.

CLICK!

WHEN I GOT OUTTA THE SLAMMER, SOMEONE HAD CALLED A MEETING OF THE BOARD.

PLEASE FOLKS, YA GOTTA UNDERSTAND!

WE'VE HEARD ENOUGH.

SECURITY?

THE SKY REALLY WAS FALLIN'!

LET'S MOVE ON. NOMINATIONS FOR OUR NEW CEO?

IN THE END, ME AND MY NUMBER TWO GUY SWITCHED PLACES. HE ADMIRES THE VIEW, AND I WATCH HIS BACK.

THE END

THE WELL-DRESSED KNIGHT

Knights of the Middle Ages were like walking tanks. Here's all the stuff they needed to put on before going into battle.

AKETON
The well-dressed knight would never wear metal against his skin. He put on this quilted jacket first. The armholes of an aketon had to be extra large so the knight could move his arms. That came in really handy when he needed to lift a lance or swing a sword.

BREECHES
Knights wore stockings under their armor. No, not the kind women wear today. These stockings (called *breeches*) were made of linen or wool. They protected a knight's legs from bruising and chaffing, the way an aketon protected his upper body.

MAIL ARMOR
The most common form of medieval armor was made of thousands of metal rings linked together. But don't call it "chain mail" unless you want a medieval scholar to laugh at you. Since "mail" means rings linked together and "chain" does, too, experts say the modern term "chain mail" is like saying the same thing twice.

HAUBERK

A knee-length mail shirt, with or without sleeves. The hauberk had to be split in the back and front, all the way to the hip. Why? So that a knight could ride a horse without his mail shirt riding up and leaving his breeches exposed to the breeze.

PLATE ARMOR

Mail armor could thwart a sword or a knife, but small arrows? Those could be a problem. One knight met defeat when an arrow sliced through his mail shirt, his mail breeches, his thigh, and even through his wooden saddle to "nail" him to his horse. Steel plates worn over mail gave a knight more protection. By A.D. 1400, the best-equipped knights wore up to 200 metal plates over their mail. The plates overlapped, covering a knight like a lobster inside its protective shell.

COIF

Think knights didn't have much under their helmets? They did. First, a knight put on a cloth cap to protect his scalp. Then he slipped on a hood made of mail called a *coif* (sounds like "quoff").

HELMET

The first helmets were like upside-down metal bowls sitting on a knight's head. Later, knights wore helmets with hinged visors to protect the entire head. Safer, but hard for a knight to see someone sneaking up on him.

GORGET

This armored collar made it impossible for a knight to bend his neck. But a stiff neck is better than a sword to the throat!

TABARD

A tabard was a sleeveless short coat worn over a knight's armor. This part of the well-dressed knight's gear showed off his coat-of-arms.

GAUNTLET

Armored gloves. Good for protecting a knight's hands, smacking a squire on the shoulder (to dub him a knight), or throwing on the ground to issue a challenge.

GREAVES

These metal plates were the part of full-body armor that covered a knight's shins. They came in pairs (Duh!).

SABATONS

A knight's feet were protected by pointy-toed metal foot covers. The longer the pointy toe, the higher the knight's ranking. The pointed toe of a noble's sabaton could be up to one foot long. A lord's could be up to two feet long. But a prince could wear sabatons of princely proportions: up to two-and-a-half feet long.

Last, but not least, what must a well-dressed knight never forget? To use the *garderobe* (the castle bathroom) *before* suiting up!

MAGICALLY DELICIOUS

An Uncle John's Totally Twisted Tale

NOT LONG AGO in a supermarket not far away, Max
hurried down the cereal aisle ahead of his mother. He
snatched a box of Sugar Gems from the shelf. Tiny
gnomes were pictured all over the box, holding fistfuls of
emerald green and ruby red Sugar Gems.

"I'd do anything for a bowl of these," Max said.
His mouth watered just thinking about it.

"Put those back, Max," said his mother as she
caught up. She grabbed a different box. "That junk will
stunt your growth. Let's stick with Vitamin Munchies."

Max made a face. "That stuff tastes like
cardboard. Please? Just this once?"

His mother ignored him as she wheeled the cart
out of the cereal aisle and turned toward the frozen
foods. Max lagged behind, staring at the gnomes on
the boxes of Sugar Gems. One of them seemed to be
staring back at him. Then it winked. "Psst! Kid!" The
gnome waved a hand. "Come here."

Max glanced over his shoulder. Was anyone else
seeing this? Max picked up the box and peered at the
waving gnome.

"How would you like to have all the Sugar Gems
you can eat?" asked the gnome.

"Is this some kind of store promotion?" Max asked.

"Uh, yeah." The gnome grinned. "Something like that."

"Then, sure," said Max. "Who wouldn't want all the Sugar Gems he could eat?"

"My thoughts exactly," said the gnome. "And it's easy as one, two, three. You ready?"

Max nodded.

"One, open this box. Two, close your eyes. And three…"

Max heard a crinkly-snapping sound. He felt himself shrinking, and then he was sliding headfirst into the box. It was like being shoved down a water slide…in the dark…with no warning. "Aaaie!" Max yelled as he slid faster and faster, whipping and whirling down, down, down into the darkness. He landed at last with a neck-jarring thunk.

Max took a deep breath and stood up. He was shaking all over, but as his eyes adjusted to the darkness, he looked around. He was in a long dark tunnel shored up with wood. The walls sparkled with red and green gems. "Wow!" Max breathed.

"Hello!" said a small squeaky voice.

Max gasped. A tiny gnome stood in front of him. And they were the same size! "Welcome to the Sugar Gem mine," said the gnome, holding out a sugary green nugget. "Eat all you want. There's plenty."

Max grabbed gems by the handful. They were delicious! He couldn't eat them fast enough. "You gnomes are really lucky," Max said. "You can eat Sugar

Gems for every meal!"

The gnome smirked. "You may think otherwise soon."

Another gnome tapped Max on the leg. "You got a quota, kid," he said. He handed Max a big cloth bag. "Fill this up. Then report to me for another."

Max took the bag. "You're making me work?"

"You have to fill ten bags a day your first week," said the boss gnome. "And double that the next week."

"I can't be here for a week!" Max said. "I'll miss school. And my mom will kill me. "

The gnome laughed. "Look, kid. You got your wish. All the Sugar Gems you can eat. In return, you work."

"And what if I don't?" Max said.

"Then you'll never go home," said the gnome in a voice that made Max's hair stand on end.

Max started filling his bag with Sugar Gems. He had to dig out the gems with his bare hands, and it took hours to fill the first bag.

"Bring that over there," the boss gnome said, pointing toward a cavernous room. Inside, dozens of gnomes were filling box after box of Sugar Gems as they sped along a conveyor belt. The belt squeaked and whirred as it moved the boxes up and out of the mine.

It took Max twice as long to fill the second bag as the first. When he dragged his second bag to the conveyer belt, he stopped to catch his breath. He watched box after box going up the belt and out of the mine. Where did they all end up? Then it hit him.

The store! Max glanced around to see if anyone was watching. The boss gnome was busy bossing the other gnomes, and they were all busy boxing Sugar Gems. Max climbed inside his bag of gems and ducked down.

He waited and waited. Finally, he felt the bag being lifted. Max heard a grunt. "Hey!" yelled a gnome. "I need a hand over here."

"The kid's a complainer," said the boss gnome. "But it feels like he mined his weight in gems."

The Sugar Gems Max had mined were poured into boxes and he slid in along with them. The box was sealed. (Luckily, the gnomes filled the boxes only halfway. That left enough air for Max to breathe.)

The box gave a jerk and started to move along the conveyer belt, climbing up and out of the mine. When the box thumped down on a shelf, Max was sure he was back in the supermarket. "Mom!" Max shouted. "Buy some Sugar Gems! Please! Sugar Gems!"

Over in the milk aisle, Max's mother had a sudden urge for Sugar Gems. She wheeled her cart back to the cereal aisle and grabbed the box. "I'll have to stash these where Max can't find them," she said.

Max could hardly wait to see his mom's face when she opened the box. He just hoped it wouldn't take too long.

Moral: Sometimes you have to think inside *the box.*

THE END

ENCHANTED EDUCATION

If Albus Dumbledore was real, and if he was really into the Internet, he might start a school like this one.

HAVE ROBE, WILL TEACH

Oberon Zell-Ravenheart has long, flowing white hair and a bushy white beard. He wears a robe sparkling with stars and trimmed in purple ribbon. And he carries a golden wand topped by a crystal globe. As Headmaster of the Grey School of Wizardry, he has been training witches and wizards since 2004. At least, that's what he claims. (He also claims to have raised unicorns and gone swimming with mermaids.) "We're an online school," says Zell-Ravenheart, called the *real* Albus Dumbledore by his fans. "And we teach all aspects of wizardry to students from age eleven up."

Zell-Ravenheart started as a traditional teacher in the 1970s, a time when many students called their teachers by their first names. He felt something was being lost in that "groovy" tradition: respect. When he opened the Grey School of Wizardry, he looked to the past for an image that would earn his students' respect. What did he find? Wizard's robes. "My wizard's outfit is basically the standard professor's outfit from the Middle Ages," he says. "If you go to a graduation at a modern university, you'll

see a bunch of people dressed exactly like that," says Zell-Ravenheart.

BITES AND BYTES

Hiring teachers with magical names also seems to be part of the headmaster's philosophy. There's Professor Moonwriter, the Dark Arts advisor. She claims family roots going back to vampires that lived in the Czech Republic. Professor Moonwriter teaches nature-based magic, outdoorcraft, herbology, and astronomy.

Professor Kalla specializes in defensive magic, energy work, and divination. She is an Eclectic Witch, and has been practicing witchcraft since 1999.

Professor LeopardDancer teaches classes on dragons and dragonlore. She has a pet dragon named Nobunaga (Well, actually…it's a python.)

And Professor Jymi X/0 is an "Urban Cybermage." Professor X/0 believes that science and math provide the keys that open the doors of magic. She has a familiar, but it isn't a cat. It's a laptop computer named TORGO.

A CURIOUS CURRICULUM

The Grey School has 16 departments, 35 teachers, and more than 200 classes. All students must begin with a class called *Ethics* to learn the rules of conduct expected in the wizarding world. After that, a budding witch or wizard has plenty of classes from which to choose.

The Department of Wizardry offers *Harry Potter 101*, taught in spring 2012 by Professor Rainmaker.

Required reading: *Harry Potter and the Sorcerer's Stone* by J.K. Rowling. Students must also have a piece of lapis lazuli (a bright blue stone). What do they learn? How the wisdom in *Harry Potter* relates to real-life wizardry.

The Department of Wortcunning (herbal wisdom) offers *Potions and Brews*. Professor Moonwriter asks students to have basic kitchen materials such as coffee filters, saucepans, measuring cups and spoons, a strainer, clean jars with screw lids, a supply of herbs, and…an adult standing by in case of emergency.

CERTIFIABLY MAGICAL

Students of the Grey School are sorted into four houses: *Sylphs, Salamanders, Undines,* and *Gnomes.* They learn rituals and spellwork, but they also learn traditional subjects such as Latin, history, geography, archaeology, and chemistry. "We teach an integration of the magical and the scientific," says the headmaster. Why? Because, he says, "Wizardry is about wisdom."

Students work their way through seven levels. Once all seven levels have been mastered, the student is awarded a certificate and the title "Journeyman Wizard."

From time to time, the Grey School of Wizardry sponsors an essay contest for kids ages 11 to 17. The topic in 2007: "Why I want to be a wizard." The winner receives a one-year scholarship, an autographed copy of the textbook *Grimoire for the Apprentice Wizard,* and a hand-crafted wand. Ready to sign up? The price of this magical education is only $30 per year.

TELL FORTUNES WITH RUNES

....

*People have used runes to predict the future
for thousands of years. It's time to see what the
runes have to say about your future.*

GET READY TO RUNE!

Before you begin, see page 92 for directions on making
your own set of runes. Start by thinking hard about a
question or problem for which you need an answer. Then
choose *one* of the following strategies:

1. Close your eyes and reach into your bag of runes. Pick
just one rune while you focus on your question. (No
peeking!)

2. Grab a handful of runes from the bag and scatter
them onto a soft surface. Pick up the rune that first
catches your eye.

3. Remove all the runes from the bag and place them
facedown. Let your hand hover over the runes. When
you feel drawn to one, pick it up and flip it over.

AND THE RUNE SAYS...

Now it's time to interpret the runes. Take the rune you've
chosen. Consult the rune chart on the next page. Think
about how the meaning of the rune or runes might apply

to the question you asked. Here's an example: You ask the runes if now's a good time to talk to your parents about something important. If you pick the rune **Ansuz**, you'll find it easy to talk to your parents. If you choose **Isa**, you'll have to work harder to get them to agree with what you want or to see your side of things. Don't worry. Each time you "read" the runes, you'll get better at interpreting them.

RUNE CHART

 Raido—Something's about to change in your life. You might be going on a journey or undertaking a quest.

 Gebo—You're about to give or receive a gift. Or maybe you'll find a new friend or fall head over heels for someone.

 Jera—Your efforts are about to pay off. You'll have peace and happiness.

 Fehu—You'll have plenty of something—luck, happiness, energy...maybe even money.

 Uruz—You'll be strong and have plenty of courage.

 Ansuz—You're smart and have things to teach others. It's easy for you to talk things over.

Wunjo—Your wishes will come true!

Isa—Something's in your way. Be patient and work harder to get what you want.

Eiwaz—The problem you've been having will be solved, and you can now move forward.

Perdo—Watch out! Things may not be what they seem.

Sowilo—If you picked this rune, you'll reach your goals.

Odal—You'll finish that project or strengthen ties with family members.

Tiwaz—You'll take the lead, as long as you're willing to put others first.

Algiz—You'll be protected from bad things.

Kenaz—You will be creative and inspired!

Blank—Expect the unexpected!

THE EMPEROR'S NEW UNDERWEAR

An Uncle John's Totally Twisted Tale

ONCE UPON A TIME, there was a very vain emperor who spent all the gold in his treasury on clothes. Then he passed sumptuary laws. What, you might ask, are sumptuary laws? Good question. Sumptuary laws say that no one can wear clothes that look more sumptuous (richer) than those worn by the guy in charge—in this case, the Very Vain Emperor.

The emperor spent most days fishing. Not for fish, which might have proved useful, but for compliments. One day, the Very Vain Emperor stood with his entire staff waiting for his carriage. "The cherries on my vest don't make me look fat, do they?" he asked the cook.

"No. You look yummy!" gushed the cook.

"And my new mink coat?" he asked his manservant. "How do I look in it?"

"Manly!" said the manservant.

Then the emperor noticed a small boy rolling out a red carpet for him. It was an important job, as the Very Vain Emperor needed to walk from the marble steps to the carriage without getting his blue silk platform shoes muddy.

"Don't you just love the way my new diamond

stickpin glitters in the sunlight?" he asked the boy.

The boy said nothing. He just kept rolling out the red carpet.

"Boy?" The emperor stopped and glared.

Knowing what had happened to the last red-carpet-rolling boy, the tailor rushed forward. "You're like a star that has fallen from the sky, majesty."

The emperor preened. "Exactly!"

"Fallen from the sky and landed on its head," the boy muttered as the carriage clattered through the castle gate. "His people got nothin' to eat but maggoty oats. And he's off buying diamond stickpins." The boy rolled up the carpet, stuck it under his arm, and stalked back inside the castle.

The tailor stood nearby, rolling and unrolling his measuring tape. The boy was right. The Very Vain Emperor had spent so much money on clothes, nothing was left for things that would benefit the people. None of the bridges the trolls had pulled down had been rebuilt. The Emperor's Road had potholes so big a princess in a pumpkin coach had been lost in one of them. And the newest book in the Royal Library? It had been chiseled in stone by a caveman named Gronk. Something had to be done.

The next day, the tailor went to work. "Sire," he said. "You must have new clothes when you tour the countryside next week."

"Indeed," said the Very Vain Emperor. "My people will look at me and see the true glory of our empire."

The tailor paid special attention to the emperor's underwear, spinning cloth as light as air and soft as kittens. Then he dyed the cloth red, the emperor's favorite color. And he sewed the most elegant pair of long johns ever seen in the empire.

As for the rest of the outfit, he searched throughout the land for clothes that showed its true glory. On the morning of the grand tour, he laid the clothes out on the emperor's bed.

"First, your undergarments, Sire!" He held up the red underwear.

"Ooh!" The emperor wriggled into them. "Light as air and soft as kittens."

Then the tailor pointed to the rest of the clothes: a farmer's mended overalls, a soldier's battle-stained jacket, and the court bard's cloak—which had gone shiny on the backside from years of sitting on it to think deep thoughts.

The Very Vain Emperor sniffed. "None of those garments are worthy of my sublime majesty." And he stalked out the door wearing nothing but his underwear.

"Behold your emperor!" He announced as he pranced down the marble staircase. "Am I not sublime?"

Everyone gasped in shock, but then quickly coughed or spluttered or hemmed or hawed as they tried to come up with compliments.

"You're sublimely...red," said one.

"Red is definitely your color, sire," said another. "Makes your cheeks glow!"

The emperor quirked one brow. "You do remember the sumptuary laws? And the penalty for being more richly dressed than your ruler?"

Everyone remembered: The penalty was losing your head. Clothes flew left and right as servants and minstrels, counts and countesses, knights and knaves stripped down to their underwear, none of which were as elegant as the emperor's new long johns.

And so the Very Vain Emperor strutted out of the castle and set off to tour his empire. In village after village, he waited for his subjects to take off their clothes, but none did. The emperor was vain, but he wasn't blind. His undies were far more sumptuous than the rags his people wore. Their clothes looked like those he'd left behind on his bed: stained, torn, mended, and so shiny on the backsides he could—and did—admire his new long johns in them.

At last, the emperor saw how his vanity had sapped the wealth of the land. He vowed that from that day forward, he would wear nothing but long johns like those the wise tailor had made for him.

And so, the empire prospered once more. Pretty soon even the poorest peasants had nice clothes. But the emperor refused to repeal the sumpturary laws. (He had his pride.) So it was no longer safe to go outside wearing anything but underwear...if you wanted to keep your head.

THE END

KNOW YOUR MYTHICAL BEASTS

Can't tell a chimera from a centaur?
Uncle John is here to help!

1. The legendary Greek chimera is part lion, part snake, and part goat. The scariest part: its breath. Why?
a. Its breath is poisonous.
b. It eats pizza with extra garlic.
c. It breathes fire.

2. The magical *stollenwurm*
a. can keep you warm in the dead of winter.
b. is a serpent-like dragon said to live in the Swiss Alps.
c. was Merlin's pet worm, stolen by the sorceress, Morgan le Fay.

3. The half-human, half-horse centaurs in C.S. Lewis's *The Chronicles of Narnia* are gifted at
a. long-distance seed spitting.
b. doing the Hokey Pokey.
c. seeing the future in the stars.

4. The Minotaur lived in a labyrinth because
a. he was too bull-headed to live in a house.
b. he thought labyrinths were a-maze-ing.
c. the King of Crete imprisoned him there.

5. The Irish believe that the banshee's cry means:
   a. Dinner!
   b. Death!
   c. Bingo!

6. In Greek legends, the hydra has nine
   a. lives.
   b. boils on its butt.
   c. heads.

7. A unicorn's horn
   a. has the power to heal.
   b. is worse than its bite.
   c. makes a great place to hang a cloak.

8. In China, dragons are thought to be
   a. dangerous near airports.
   b. good luck.
   c. bad dinner guests.

9. The Romans once thought fauns would sneak into
   a. your bedroom at night and give you nightmares.
   b. movies without paying.
   c. your fridge and eat all the leftovers.

10. In Japan, the kappa is a legendary water goblin that
   a. loses its strength when it bows politely.
   b. likes to eat human livers.
   c. both a and b.

Answers on page 286.

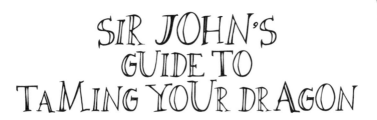

SIR JOHN'S GUIDE TO TAMING YOUR DRAGON

*The toughest part of taming a dragon is finding
a dragon's egg. Oh, and the singed eyebrows.*

1. Taming must begin before your dragon hatches. Keep
the dragon's egg warm by wedging it into your armpit.
Hold the egg there until the hatchling starts ripping
through the shell with its egg tooth—the sharp bone
on its snout. *Be patient!* It will take up to 36 months for
your dragon egg to hatch.

2. Sing to your egg once an hour. *Do not neglect this
step!* You may annoy your teachers, but remember—a
wild dragon is harder to handle than an angry teacher
(most of the time).

3. When your egg starts to hatch, kick everyone else
out of the room. The hatchling will bond with the first
person it sees. If your dragon doesn't nudge you with
its snout and start to purr, you may want to run. Those
tiny teeth and claws are needle-sharp.

4. Be sure to have a mound of fresh raw meat on hand.
(Hamburger will do.) Your dragon will be starving

when it hatches. It must have fresh meat right away, and if you forget the meat, your fingers will do just fine. (If you have fingers after this step, wash them with soapy water before putting them in your mouth. Raw meat is good for dragons, but not for dragon tamers.)

5. Dragon language consists of hisses, snorts, and friendly nips. Unfortunately, the nips can leave nasty scars on humans. So read bedtime stories to your hatchling. The more stories you read, the quicker it will learn to speak human language.

6. Once your hatchling understands you, you can teach it to breathe fire, hunt for food, and—if you're very patient—poop outside your "cave." Dragonlings learn best by imitation, so demonstrate what you want your dragon to do, and it will happily copy you.

7. It's almost impossible to tell a male dragonling from a female. Dragon tamers have lost fingers, eyes, and even noses trying to find out. The safest way to determine if you have a male or female dragon? Ask. If the dragon thinks you need to know, he (or she) will tell you.

8. It takes a year for your dragon's scales to harden, so it will be up to you to protect it from roving knights. Your dragon will be watching. The more knights you chase away, the more it will trust you (and the less likely it will be to eat you if you forget to feed it).

SECRET ARTS
OF THE NINJAS

*Fact: Teenage mutant ninja turtles are not real. But ninjas?
They've been around for centuries. And if you haven't seen
one, it's because they don't want you to see them.*

WARLORDS VS. PEASANTS

Tracing ninja history is like trying to catch smoke in
your hand. The first ninjas probably lived in the rugged
mountains of Japan's largest island—Honshu—about
1,100 years ago. Those were tough times for common
people. Peasants often got caught in the cross fire
between Japan's powerful warlords.

Simple mountain villagers stood no chance against
a warlord's powerful army. So they developed *ninjitsu*,
a form of guerrilla warfare. Guerrilla warfare lets small
forces take on big armies, often by using hit-and-run
tactics. Ninjas learned to spy, to sabotage, and—when
necessary—to kill. Over time, they not only learned to
defend themselves, they became Japan's stealthiest and
most feared assassins.

WHO PUT THE "NIN" IN NINJA?

Japan's ninjas learned the skills they needed from many
sources. From Chinese warriors they learned stealth,
resourcefulness, and adaptability. From Buddhist monks,

they learned body conditioning and the use of potions. From Chinese pirates, they learned spying, sudden strikes, and spreading fear. And from their own people? They learned to observe nature and imitate plants and animals.

HIDE AND SNEAK

Need to hide? Act like a quail and hunker down in small gaps between bushes. Don't want to be seen? Climb a tree like a raccoon (people almost never look up). Enemy headed your way? Curl up in a ball and "hide like a stone." Ninjas became so skilled at using nature's tricks that soon rumors about their "special powers" began to spread.

People claimed to have seen ninjas walking on water, passing through solid walls, disappearing into thin air, and even changing into demons. Many Japanese believed ninjas were ghosts, sent to Earth to kill humans. Rumor has it that ninjas spread many of these tales themselves. Why? They knew that frightened enemies usually run away instead of fighting.

OFF TO CAMP

If you were born into a Japanese ninja family, you could begin training at age five. Both boys and girls could train, but where? After all, ninja kids had to keep what they learned secret from non-ninja kids. The solution: Ninja parents sent their kids to camp—ninja training camp. These camps were hidden deep in the mountains.

At camp, ninja kids learned to leap from tree to tree, to climb the walls of buildings, and to cling to ceilings like flies. They learned to use weapons: throwing stars, links of chain, short swords, daggers, darts, and caltrops—big metal jacks with sharp points. (Ever step on a jack with bare feet?) Most of all, they learned "the art of stealth," because a ninja's most important job was to spy on enemies.

Stealth means being so sneaky no one knows you're there. To avoid being seen, ninja kids learned to walk silently and to wear black clothes that blended into the night. And they learned to carry powders made of ashes, pepper, and sand that could temporarily blind an enemy. (Can you see me now?)

INVISIBLE ME

Ninjas also used disguises to make themselves "invisible." To sneak into a camp, village, or household without being spotted, a ninja couldn't just put on a costume. He had to *become* someone else. Ninjas had seven main disguises to help them blend in: traveling priest, wandering samurai, musician, merchant, mountain warrior, entertainer, and Buddhist monk.

To be truly invisible, the ninja had to walk, talk, work, eat, play—even go to the bathroom—like the character he was pretending to be. A ninja didn't have to stick to one of the traditional cover roles, but he did have to chose each role carefully and make sure that nothing would give him away. Smooth hands could betray a

young ninja if he tried to disguise himself as an elderly farmer. And a ninja grandmother's wrinkles would give her away if she tried to pass as a schoolgirl.

A DEADLY HAND

Ninjas traveled lightly, carrying only what they needed. Their pockets might hold small weapons, a rope, dried food, medicine, packets of "blinding powder," and claws made of leather and iron to help them climb walls. But even if their pockets were empty, ninjas always had their most effective weapons: their bodies.

Ninjas learned to fight with their hands, feet, elbows, knees…even their shoulders. Some ninjas were said to be able to pull Earth's energy into their hands. With one wave of the "Vibrating Palm," such a ninja could strike an enemy dead without even touching him.

CATCH AND RELEASE

No matter how hard ninjas fought, sometimes they were captured. But ninjitsu is also "the art of escaping." If a ninja found himself trapped on a boat, he could dive overboard. He could stay underwater for hours, breathing through a shallow reed until his captors gave up the search.

Even when bound by ropes, a ninja could often get away. How? First, the ninja would stretch the tissue that connected two of his bones. Then he could pop the bone out of its socket. (Ouch!) Dislocating a bone loosened the ropes just enough for the ninja to slip free.

To complete an escape, ninjas could open locks without keys or disappear in a puff of smoke. They could even pull snakes out of their sleeves and "vanish" while their enemies were screaming and running away.

IT'S A BIRD, IT'S A PLANE, IT'S...

While Japan's warlords fought it out, the ninjas' "magical" fighting skills were in high demand. Powerful warlords hired them to spy on enemies. And noble samurai warriors—whose code of honor forced them to fight in the open—hired them to fight from the shadows.

Both the warlords and the samurai are now part of Japan's colorful history. As for ninjas? Their secret arts are still taught and still fiercely guarded. So if you're out for a stroll and feel a shiver between your shoulders, don't forget to look up!

o   o   o

Raj: Now, what can you buy your homeless friend for Christmas? I have a box full of Teenage Mutant Ninja Turtles stationery sets I can't seem to shift.

Chloe: I'm not sure a tramp really has any *need* for a Teenage Mutant Ninja Turtle stationery set.

—from *Mr. Stink* by David Walliams

"Wise man say, 'Forgiveness is divine, but never pay full price for late pizza.'"

—Michelangelo, Teenage Mutant Ninja Turtle

THE PLATYPUS PRINCE

An Uncle John's Totally Twisted Tale

ONCE UPON A TIME...in a faraway kingdom, there lived a handsome prince and a horrid, wicked witch. The witch had an ingrown toenail that hurt so much it made it impossible to be nice. Instead of making a doctor's appointment—like a normal person would— the witch took out her pain on everyone else.

One day while the prince was out taking a walk, he accidentally stepped on the witch's toe—the one with the ingrown nail. The pain was so bad the witch's eyes crossed. But she still managed to cast a spell that turned the prince into a platypus.

Now a platypus, as everyone knows, is a furry pudgy creature with flippers instead of hands and a huge duck's bill. The prince was not happy. "Why would you do such a thing?" he asked.

"My toe feels like it's going to explode!" wailed the witch.

"I'm terribly sorry!" said the prince. He would have gotten down on his knees to plead with the witch, but, as everyone also knows, a platypus does not have knees. "Please, make me human again!"

By then, the witch's toenail pain was down to a

dull throb. "Fine." She snapped her fingers.

The prince looked down at himself with his beady black platypus eyes. "Still a platypus," he said.

The witch grinned. "For the counterspell to work, you have to get a girl to kiss you."

"A girl? Any girl?" The platypus prince scratched his pudgy belly with his claws. "I thought it had to be a princess."

"I'm lowering my standards," said the witch.

So Prince Platypus wandered the countryside, taking dips in swamps and looking for a girl to kiss him. But even the girls who believed his story couldn't get past the fact that his breath now smelled like swamp gas.

Every so often, Prince Platypus ran into the witch. And every time he saw her, she was turning someone else into something non-human. The prince knew he had to stop her, so he went to the doctor—the only one in the kingdom. He thought he'd have to wait for hours, but she called him in right away.

Prince Platypus explained his plan. The doctor acted like she was listening, but really she was thinking about how slow business had been lately. Most of her patients had been turned into animals and were now going to the local vet.

When the prince stopped talking, she wrote him a prescription for painkillers and told him to come back in a week for a follow-up.

"Wait!" he said. "I don't think you understand."

The prince explained his plan again. This time

the doctor actually listened. "Just might work," she said. She picked up the phone and called the witch. "There's a platypus in my office claiming to be the prince," she said. "He says you're the only one who can verify his identity, and I need to bill his insurance. Could you come to my office right away?" Then she hung up and filled a syringe with knock-out juice.

Prince Platypus took one look at the shot needle and started to sway.

"Put your head between your knees," said the doctor, forgetting that platypuses don't have knees.

The prince closed his eyes instead. A few minutes later, he heard something that sounded like a witch flying in through an open window. Then he heard something that sounded like a scuffle. Then he heard a teakettle shrieking, but it was the witch screeching because the doctor hadn't waited for the knock-out juice to take effect before removing the ingrown toenail.

When things got quiet, Prince Platypus opened his eyes. The horrible toenail was out.

"What do I owe you?" the witch asked.

"Nothing," said the doctor. "The platypus is paying."

The witch was so happy to be pain-free that she kissed the platypus right on the bill. And he turned back into a prince.

The witch looked at the doctor for a minute. "Actually, I think I do owe you something," she said. And with one finger snap, she turned the doctor into an almiqui. You probably don't know anything about those, since the species has been extinct for years. Imagine a woolly mammoth that's about a foot tall. It has a long ratty nose and pointy rat's teeth. In fact, imagine a woolly mammoth rat.

"Next time you remove an ingrown toenail," said the witch, "wait for the knock-out juice to kick in."

THE END

o o o

WORLD'S WEIRDEST ANIMALS

Now that you're worried about being turned into a weird animal by a witch, here are a few real-life possibilities!

- **Aye-ayes** live on the island of Madagascar off the southeastern coast of Africa. They're primates (so are monkeys) with shaggy fur, round staring eyes, and batlike ears. Their fingers look a lot like twigs with claws on the ends. And their middle fingers are bonier and longer than the others. Why? The better to pick grubs out of tree bark and eat them, my dear.

- **Naked-neck chickens** come from Transylvania (legendary home of Count Dracula). They have feathered bodies like other chickens. But their necks? Those are long, skinny, and featherless, with bright

pink skin that looks like it's just been plucked. It hasn't. The chicks come out of their shells with naked necks.

- **Sucker-footed bats** (also from Madagascar) have round pads at the ends of their wrists and ankles instead of fingers or toes. Why? So they can roost right-side up instead of upside down like other bats. The pads secrete sticky sweat, and it's the sweat that makes the pads act like suction cups. One expert says they shouldn't be called sucker-footed bats at all. They should be called wet-adhesion bats. (Really?)

- **Golden-rumped elephant shrews** rumble around the dry coastal forests of Kenya, Africa, searching through leaves with their long, pointed, bendy snouts. What are they looking for? Millipedes, spiders, and earthworms to gobble up. The biggest of these shrews are about the size of a small cat, so they rely on their absolutely huge bottoms for protection. How can big bottoms help? The skin is extra-thick. If a predator bites into one of those tough bottoms, its teeth may not make a dent.

- **Yellow dung flies** (wherever there's poop) have furry yellow bodies and legs, and bulging red eyes. They spend their whole lives either buzzing around looking for poop or living in it. As adults, they dine on insects, but when they're just babies (larvae), they eat dung. Their favorite meals? Cowpats or horse droppings.

Three Silly Huntsmen

by Valeri Gorbachev

One day, the three silly huntsmen went to the North Pole.

FAIRY
IDENTIFICATION
GUIDE

*If you can't tell one fairy from another, you could be
in serious trouble during a fairy invasion.
Arm yourself with the facts before that happens!*

LEPRECHAUNS

Irish lore says that leprechauns are part of a fairy group
known as *Luacharma'n*, meaning "little people." Over
time the name has been confused with the Irish word
leath-bhrogan, "maker-of-a-shoe." Whether or not
leprechauns are actually shoemakers has been hotly
debated for centuries. But everyone agrees that they have
plenty of gold and they're not about to share it. You can
recognize leprechauns by their trademark red hair and
pointed hats. They are rarely cooperative and always
place a higher priority on amusing themselves than on
helping humans.

GOBLINS

The Welsh word *coblyn* means both *thumper* and *fiend*.
Some believe it is the original word for goblin. Welsh
miners describe the *coblynau* as small fairies who live
in the mines, caves, and other secret places in the
mountains. They're about a foot and a half tall and very

ugly. In fact, some say they're the most hideous creatures you'll ever see. Their faces can look like animals, ugly birds, or even insects. Goblins have a mean streak and have been known to throw stones at miners. But their presence is thought to bring good luck.

DWARFS

The Germans tell of mountain dwarfs who live in underground halls heaped with gold and sparkling jewels. Most are no taller than a two-year-old kid, but they look more like old men with stooped backs and long, flowing beards. Their ancestors worked as miners, so modern dwarfs often have jobs that let them work with their hands. Legends say that dwarfs come from a realm called *Svart-alfa-heim* (Dark Elves' Home). Like other dark elves, they must avoid the sun or risk being turned to stone.

PIXIES

A pixie is a farm or household spirit common in western England. Folklore says they're usually earthy green with pointy ears, wings, and heads that are way too big for their tiny bodies. Pixies serve their hosts well. But if a farmer or householder is lazy, sloppy, or ungrateful, watch out! Pixies like to pinch! If you get on the wrong side of a pixie, try offering its favorite meal: bread and cheese.

WATER FAIRIES

These fairies have been sighted all over the world, from Scotland to Greece to New Zealand. Water fairies come in all shapes and sizes and include mermaids, shellycoats, sirens, undines, kelpies (water horses), and selkies. They sometimes help lost sailors reach safety or fishermen catch fish. But most water fairies split their time between searching for human mates, luring people to their doom, and fiercely guarding their homes. If you're hanging around a river, stream, lake, pond, sea, ocean—or even a puddle—watch out for these dangerous creatures.

ELVES

Nordic myth divides elves into two types: light elves and dark elves. The light elves have pearly pale skin and flit about on gossamer wings. The dark elves live below ground and are land-bound. (No wings!) Most elves have pointed ears. But they may cover them up with large hats that look like mushrooms. They can be found in fields and woods, but they're shyer than other fairy types. Avoid sudden movement or loud noises if you want to befriend an elf. And don't go elf-hunting with your cat! Cats have been known to bite off their heads.

BOGGARTS

Also known as bogeymen or boogiemen, boggarts are said to have come to England from Germany (along with the trolls). They are lonely, repulsive, and mean. Because they can shape-shift, it's hard to recognize a boggart. But they are known to egg on bullies and bratty kids, and to spread gossip, lies, and rumors. If you see such behavior, a boggart is probably nearby. Contact is not advised!

WITCH WIT

When a witch tells a joke, laugh.
Even if it's not funny.

Q: What do you call a
witch who's been hit by a
shrinking spell?
A: Dot.

WITCH: I'd like a black cat
for my son.
PET STORE OWNER:
Sorry. We don't do
trades.

Q: Why won't witches go
to the beach?
A: They don't want to
turn into sandwiches.

Q: Why didn't the witch
send text messages?
A: She couldn't spell.

Q: How do you make a
witch itch?
A: Take away her *w*.

Q: How many witches
does it take to change a
lightbulb?
A: It depends on what you
want to change it into.

Q: Why do witches cover
their mouths when they
sneeze?
A: To catch their false
teeth.

UMPIRE: Batter up!
WITCH: Sorry. We can't
catch the bats.

Q: How does a witch
protect her potions?
A: With a warlock.

Q: What is a witch's
favorite pet?
A: A wart hog.

COMMON CENTS

*Alchemy is the process of turning cheap metals
(like lead or iron) into precious ones (like gold or silver).
Here's the thing: it doesn't work. But you can change the
look of some metals, right in your kitchen.*

WHAT YOU NEED:

- 20 dull pennies. (Look for pennies dated 1982 or earlier. Before that year, pennies were made almost entirely of copper. Since then, they've been made by pouring a thin layer of copper over a zinc core. This experiment will usually work with the newer pennies, too, unless they have scratches that expose the zinc.)
- ¼ cup of white vinegar
- 1 teaspoon of salt
- Shallow plastic or glass bowl (not metal)
- Paper towels
- A few metal nails or screws

WHAT TO DO:

1. Put the salt and vinegar into the bowl. Stir until the salt has dissolved.
2. Dip a penny halfway into the mix. Hold it there for about 10 seconds. See any difference in the two halves?
3. Place the rest of the pennies into the bowl. Leave them for 5 minutes.
4. Remove half the pennies. Put them on a paper towel.

5. Remove the rest of the pennies. Rinse them under running water. Put them on another paper towel.

6. Check the pennies in about an hour. In the meantime, put a nail in the leftover liquid. Rest another nail against the inside of the bowl so half of it is in the vinegar mixture and half is out.

THE SCIENCE

The dull coating on old pennies is *copper oxide*. Copper oxide forms when copper atoms combine with oxygen atoms in the air. What's an atom? It's a tiny particle. You can't see atoms with the naked eye, but everything in the world is made up of them.

When the pennies are put into a weak acid such as vinegar, the copper oxide dissolves. Chlorine atoms from the salt mix with the copper atoms and the oxygen atoms to make a compound called *malachite*, which is bluish-green. The unrinsed pennies turn greenish because of the malachite. Rinsing the pennies stops this process, so those pennies don't turn green.

The copper atoms left behind in the vinegar coat the steel nails. That makes the nails *look* like copper, but only on the outside.

MORE METAL MADNESS

○ Use lemon juice or orange juice instead of vinegar.
○ See if adding more or less salt makes a difference.
○ Put pennies into ketchup instead of salt and vinegar.
○ Try the experiment on nickels or dimes.

ALI BABA
AND THE FORTY
STEVES

....

An Uncle John's Totally Twisted Tale

ONCE UPON A TIME there was a kid named Ali
Baba. Ali Baba lived in an apartment between a skate
park and a pizza parlor, which he thought was totally
gnarly. Then one day, his parents told him they had
good news.

"Dad got a better job," said his mom. "So we're
moving to the suburbs."

"What? No way!" To Ali Baba, that sounded like
a fate worse than road rash. So he did what he always
did when he needed to think. He grabbed his board
and headed to the skate park.

It was packed. All these guys with straight black
hair wearing silk pajama bottoms and embroidered
vests had taken over the park. They looked like extras
from a movie about *The Arabian Nights*, but they could
skate. One of them was doing a noseslide off a stair
rail. One did a perfect McTwist down the ramp. And
another one caught enough air coming off the quarter
pipe to get a nosebleed.

The pajama guys all seemed to know each other.
Ali Baba couldn't make out everything they were

saying, but they kept calling each other Steve.

"Hey, Steve," said one. "You seriously ollied that twelve-step!"

"Thanks, Steve," said a guy by the stairs.

"I don't know, Steve," said a third guy. "Looked a little sketchy to me."

"Steve! You're just jealous," said the ollie Steve.

Ali Baba was fascinated by the crew of Steves. One of them noticed him staring and yelled, "Hey! You a local?"

"Yeah," said Ali Baba. "At least for now."

"I'm Steve," said the first Steve, sticking out his hand.

"Steve!" said the next.

"And I'm Steve," said a third.

One by one, Ali Baba shook hands with the Steves and counted them—thirty-nine in all. *Thirty-nine Steves!* Ali Baba could hardly believe it. "I'm Ali Baba," he said. "How do all you Steves tell each other apart?"

"Easy," said Steve.

It didn't seem easy to Ali Baba. In fact, he had no idea if it was Steve #1 or Steve #39 who had answered.

"By looks," said Steve. "That's Steve with the Wart." He pointed to a Steve with the most flawless skin Ali Baba had ever seen. "That's Bald Steve." He nodded toward a Steve with thick black hair. "Steve with the sick skateboard." The Steve he pointed to did have an awesome board, but so did the other thirty-eight Steves. After all the Steves had identified themselves (giving Ali Baba a massive headache), he decided to tell them about his parents' plan to move to the burbs.

"You'll just have to stop them," said the Steves.

Ali Baba shook his head. "How? You guys got a genie in a magic bottle or something?" The Steves laughed nervously, and then they hustled Ali Baba toward the pizza parlor to cheer him up.

A few days later, Ali Baba was packing random skateboard junk into a box when the doorbell rang. He dropped some spare bearings into the box and ran to press the intercom buzzer. "Yeah?" he said.

"It's Steve!" a voice echoed through the intercom.

"And Steve!"

"And, dude! Don't forget Steve!"

"Okay, okay," said Ali Baba. "I get it. Come on. I'll buzz you up."

The Steves thumped up the stairs. When Ali Baba opened the door, all thirty-nine of them crowded into his tiny apartment. Then one of them dumped a canvas bag at Ali Baba's feet. "We found what you needed."

"Huh?" said Ali Baba, peering into the sack. Inside was a dented teakettle. "Uh…thanks?"

Steve with the Wart (or at least the Steve with the best skin) pulled the kettle from the sack. "You asked for a genie. And your wish is our command. All you gotta do is rub the kettle and say the magic word."

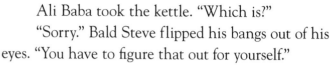

Ali Baba took the kettle. "Which is?"

"Sorry." Bald Steve flipped his bangs out of his eyes. "You have to figure that out for yourself."

Ali Baba looked from Steve to Steve to Steve to Steve…and so on. By the time he got to about the twentieth Steve, he'd started nervously rubbing the teakettle with his thumb. "Look, Steve—" he said.

Ali Baba stopped. Smoke had started gushing out of the kettle's spout. It formed into the shape of a man with a round belly and then, *Pop!* The figure came to life in a burst of fireworks.

"Master." The round-bellied man bowed. "You summoned me with the magic word. And your wish is my command."

Ali Baba blinked. "What magic word?"

"My name." The genie grinned. "Steve!"

Ali Baba's eyes widened. "And I get a wish?"

The genie bowed again. "Of course, master!"

Ali Baba knew exactly what he wanted. "I wish to be eighteen years old so I can stay right here when my parents move."

"Easy peasy," said the genie, snapping his plump fingers.

And that, my friends, is how thirty-nine Steves became forty Steves. And how Ali Baba was able to live happily ever after in an apartment between a skate park and a pizza parlor.

THE END

A POX UPON THEE!

May you never need a magical curse. But just in case…
here are a few of our favorites.

May the desert wind blow
angry scorpions up your robe.

May malevolent hedgehogs
soil your cornflakes.

May you be swallowed by a
whale with bad breath.

May the dog really eat your
homework.

May you be trapped in an
elevator with the world
farting champion.

May a family of ferrets
nest in your knickers.

May the fleas of a
thousand camels
infest your armpits.

May your gastric juices
keep you from sleeping
at night.

May you grow like an
onion…with your head in
the ground.

May no one tell you about
the spinach
between your teeth.

May you be smitten with
an itch where you cannot
scratch.

May you find a half-eaten
worm in your apple…
after you swallow.

May the lumps in your
oatmeal hide cockroaches.

ANSWER PAGE

Find the Fart Fairy (page x)

At last count, the fart fairy showed up 17 times in the book (pages i, vi, vii, ix, x, 12, 36, 60, 86, 130, 170, 210, 256, 286, and 288). If you found them all, you win an official Fart Fairy Magic Raspberry. Here it is—*Pfhtttttttt!*

Riddle Me This (page 32)

Chomping at the Bit—teeth; This Girl Is Hot!—a candle; The Yolk Is on You—an egg; Tug of Water—a well.

The Shoemaker and the Elvis Impersonators (page 39)

I'm All Shook Up; Don't Be Cruel; Hound Dog; Heartbreak Hotel; Runaway; Don't Think Twice, It's All Right; and, of course, *Blue Suede Shoes*.

The White Queen's Riddle (page 64)

Answer: An oyster. It's a sea creature that can't swim. A penny would buy one in Carroll's day. It cooks quickly and lies in its own dish. One is not enough to fill you up, so set at least a "score" (20) on your table. And the "dish-cover"? That's the oyster shell. You must open it with a knife to un-dish-cover the oyster in the middle.

Prince Charming's Latin Lesson (page 113)

1. b; 2. c; 3. e; 4. d; 5. f; 6. a.

Alchemical Facts and Fakes (page 184)

Believe it or not, statements 2, 4, 5, and 6 have been thought to be true. We made up statements 1 and 3.

Know Your Mythical Beasts (page 257)

1. c; 2. b; 3. c; 4. c; 5. b; 6. c; 7. a; 8. b; 9. a; 10. c.

Uncle John's Bathroom Readers
FOR KIDS ONLY!

To order, contact: **Bathroom Readers' Press**
P.O. Box 1117, Ashland, OR, 97520
Or visit us online at www.bathroomreader.com

THE LAST PAGE

FELLOW BATHROOM READERS: Bathroom reading should never be taken loosely, so Sit Down and Be Counted! Join the Bathroom Readers' Institute. Just go to www.bathroomreader.com to sign up. It's free! Or send a self-addressed, stamped envelope and your email address to: Bathroom Readers' Institute, P.O. Box 1117, Ashland, Oregon 97520. You'll receive a free membership card, our BRI newsletter (sent out via email), discounts when ordering directly through the BRI, and a permanent spot on the BRI honor roll!

UNCLE JOHN'S NEXT BATHROOM READER FOR KIDS ONLY IS ALREADY IN THE WORKS!

Is there a subject you'd like to read about in our next Uncle John's Bathroom Reader for Kids Only? Go to CONTACT US at www.bathroomreader.com and let us know. We aim to please.

Well, we're out of space, and when you've got to go, you've got to go. Hope to hear from you soon. Meanwhile, remember…

GO WITH THE FLOW!